Wages and Employment in the E. E. C.

P–E Briefing Guides to E.E.C.

The enlargement of the European Economic Community from the original six countries to nine will create new opportunities for companies both in and out of the Community.

But it will also create problems and, above all, a need for sound and authoritative information and advice.

The books in the *P–E Briefing Guide* series have each been written by a subject expert, in collaboration with the P–E Consulting Group Ltd.

Each Guide takes a specific topic, vital to a company's dealings in the E.E.C., and provides the basic information the operating manager needs to have.

The first five titles in the series are:

Wages and Employment in the E.E.C. *D.D. Jones*
Restrictive Practices and Monopolies in E.E.C. Law
James P. Cunningham
Transport and Delivery to European Customers *David Lowe*
Marketing in the E.E.C. *Gordon J. Bolt*
Communicating with E.E.C. Customers *Gordon J. Bolt*

P. E. Briefing Guide to:

Wages and Employment in the E. E. C.

dewi-davies jones

Kogan Page

10 SEP. 1973

DR
331.294

First published 1973
By Kogan Page Limited,
116a Pentonville Road, London N1 9JN

Copyright © by dewi-davies jones 1973

Typesetting by Gyro Repro Limited,
Hockers Lane, Detling, Kent
Printed by Compton Printing Limited,
Aylesbury and London

SBN 85038 027 8 P/B
   85038 039 1 H/B 7403

Contents

Introduction

In the fifteen years since the E.E.C. was set up, systems of industrial relations and labour law have remained as widely different as they ever were before. Differences in cultural, social and political attitudes and traditions have brought about widely differing systems; and despite the broadly-framed 'social provisions' of the Treaty of Rome, the European Communities have only recently started to approach the question of harmonization of labour law and industrial relations structures in an active way.

During this time the situation in the member countries of the Six and of the Nine has not stood still. In every European country, the last decade has seen changes whose implications are at least as far-reaching as those of the Industrial Relations Act and the other major legislation enacted in the United Kingdom. Nevertheless, growing European integration has meant that individual countries increasingly look around them before making internal changes, and in more than one area national approaches to problems have been similar to the approaches of other countries.

For this reason, the present book attempts firstly to describe briefly some of the main features of industrial relations in 9 countries; secondly to list the provisions of the Treaty of Rome and the intentions which the Community institutions have in respect of future 'European' industrial relations policy; and thirdly to note the probable effects of E.E.C. entry on UK industrial relations.

The largest sections are those on Germany, France and Italy, whose size and industrial structure most nearly compares with Britain's. Industrial (and social) relationships differ widely in all nine countries, however, and the shorter sections (on the smaller countries) draw attention to the main parallels and differences. Nevertheless, the information can only represent a beginning. Industrial relations are closely tied up with the social and political structure of a country; there are many seemingly irrelevant factors in everyday life which may be of major importance in determining the course of a country's industrial life. Nothing should be taken for granted; direct comparisons are liable to be misleading.

The following chapters represent an introduction to the major characteristics of different countries, stressing the areas in which the Community may be interested (for the purposes of harmonization) and those details which may be of interest to, for example, British managers. The book cannot hope to be definitive in its description, but it may serve a briefing function when trying to evaluate which will be the problems facing industry in Europe in the next few years.

It is still possible that Norway may soon join the Community. For this reason details of Norway are included at the end of the book.

Part 1. The Countries

1. Germany

Labour market

In 1970, the active German working population was about 27 million, of whom 8% worked in agriculture, 49% industry, 31.3% services and 10.7% civil servants. The major labour market trends showed a continuing decline in agricultural employment, in coal-mining, textiles and shipbuilding. Increases in employment in chemicals (particularly plastics) and mechanical engineering have been consistent over the last ten years.

Over the past fifteen years, however, Germany has combined high growth rates — both industrially and in terms of real incomes — with a level of unemployment well under 1% (currently 0.6%) and a growing number of foreign workers, now nearing 2 million. Of the foreign workers only about 200,000 come from Six countries, mainly Italy. The rest are from Germany's traditional sources: Greece, Turkey, Yugoslavia, Bulgaria and Romania. Unemployment is highest in the Saar, and the less industrial areas; but in the industrial Länder — North-Rhine/Westphalia, Rhineland-Palatinate, Baden-Württemberg, Hessen, Lower Saxony — there is a shortage of skilled workers, and the labour market remains tight for specialised and semi-skilled labour, and this is reflected in wage-levels. (The Federal Government has passed a law expanding vocational training facilities, but this is unlikely to have any short-term effect.)

Employment

Recruitment

Theoretically, recruitment is the responsibility of the state employment service. In practice employers hire labour independently of the service, in the ways familiar to British employers (advertisement etc.). Nevertheless, the German employer is obliged to keep the local employment office informed, within 3 days, of all engagements and dismissals.

The employment office must be informed in a variety of circumstances — it can delay dismissals in redundancies involving more than 50 employees; it must be informed of dismissals on construction sites due to bad weather; it must be informed of labour disputes.

Establishments employing more than 15 (and this applies to each individual establishment of a company) are required to reserve 6% of jobs for seriously disabled workers — i.e. with up to 50% disability. The employer must apply to the employment office: failure to comply with their requirements may incur the obligatory employment of disabled workers designated by the authorities, or a fine.

Foreign workers require a work permit and a residence permit; it is necessary to obtain an entry visa first. Although the applicant is obliged to ,obtain these for himself, a note from the German employer to the effect that a job is available and cannot be filled from local resources can help to speed the process. E.E.C. nationals require only a passport or identity card for entry, and residence is permitted on the 'permit for citizens of an E.E.C. member State', given initially for five years and renewable.

Employment premiums. It is, in some cases, possible to obtain State subsidies for the construction of housing for employees. There are also a number of other premiums; for example, for employing workers who have been long unemployed, a subsidy of up to 50% of remuneration may be paid for up to 6 months.

Involvement of the Works Council. The Works Council has a right to require that vacant jobs be advertised within the plant before being offered outside. If internal transfers are made as a result, the Works Council has to agree to the personnel selected. It can also object to individual new engagements.

Individual rights of the employee. The Works Constitution Act has laid down a series of statutory rights for individuals. The employer is bound to explain to the employee the nature of his job and his responsibilities, the nature of his activities and their relation to the overall structure and function of the undertaking. For this reason, a firm needs to have available a set of job descriptions. If there is overall job evaluation, it must be borne in mind that the Works Council has a right of co-decision in determining the basic principles of the system used. The employee must also be made aware of dangers inherent in his job.

The employee must also be instructed in the calculation and make-up of his pay; again, the Works Council has a say in domestic payment systems.

Finally, the employee has a right to inspect any personal file which may be kept on him: and he may demand clarification of its contents. In such a case, any notes of clarification — which the employer is obliged to provide — must be appended to the file.

Contract of employment

The form. A contract of employment exists where anybody undertakes to perform work personally for an employer: therefore, except in certain specific cases, it does not have to be in written form, but can be concluded verbally or by a conclusive act. Written contracts are required for apprentices, however; and for agricultural workers who are to be employed for more than six months (this is because payment in kind is included; also, they are not covered by any collective agreement). Special agreements made within ordinary contracts of employment may require to be in separate, written form (e.g., clauses barring competition for commercial representatives fall into this category).

Content. The German contract of employment — i.e. the 'employment relationship' — includes a wide variety of implied terms, arising from law, collective agreements or custom and practice. In itself, the contract requires employer and employees to observe certain fundamental rights and obligations. The employee is obliged

- to work (but also to be provided with work)
- to be loyal
- to follow instructions

and the employer is obliged
- to pay wages
- to ensure the safety and welfare of his employee
- to comply with legislation (e.g. to allow minimum paid holidays; to operate schemes for capital formation)

All these obligations are implicitly qualified by specific legislation or collective agreements. The *method* of payment, for example, is not at the employer's discretion: it is subject to legal and collectively agreed norms and to the Works Council's right of co-decision.

If personal details are included in a standard written contract format, the agreement of the Works Council is required.

Termination of contract — dismissal — redundancy. The 'employment relationship' can be terminated:

(i)   By agreement between the parties.
(ii) By expiry, in the case of a fixed-term contract or by completion of the job or service, if it is a contract of work.
(iii) By the death of the employee.
(iv) By either party giving notice, if the contract is of indefinite duration. (The employee is then entitled to a reasonable period of time off to look for another job.)

The law distinguishes two types of termination:

— ordinary termination, in which case the legal or collectively agreed periods of notice must be observed
— extraordinary termination, which may involve summary dismissal: it does not however exclude the possibility of notice, either full or reduced. §626 of the Civil Code states 'The employment relationship may be terminated by either party without notice for an important reason if a situation arises in which the party terminating the relationship cannot, on consideration of all the circumstances of the individual case and taking into account the interests of both parties, reasonably be expected to continue the relationship to the end of the period of notice or to the agreed date of expiry of the contract'. The important reason may be: constant breach of a fundamental obligation; personal insult; serious breach of confidence, etc.
   Termination must be effected within two weeks of the 'situation' arising; on demand, the grounds for such termination must be given in writing.

Notice does not, in principle, need to be given in writing, except where collective agreements specify to the contrary, but it is probably advisable to give it in written form, together with the grounds. The Works Constitution Act requires the Works Council to be informed in advance of all dismissals and of the reasons. If it objects to an ordinary dismissal, it must give its reasons in writing within a week, otherwise it is deemed to have assented. In extraordinary dismissals it must raise objections within 3 days.
   Dismissal of an employee over 18 who has been employed for at least 6 months is *null* if the dismissal is 'socially unjustifiable'. §1 of the Protection Against Dismissal Act defines this as 'dismissal for reasons which do not lie in the person or the behaviour of the employee (e.g. acts which would justify summary dismissal), or in

urgent requirements of the firm which prevent the continued employment of the employee'. The onus of proof lies with the employee.

A dismissal is also socially unjustifiable if

— the employer has failed to take social considerations into account in selecting the employee for dismissal or redundancy;
— the dismissal conflicts with the guidelines for selection which each firm is required to establish subject to the Works Council's agreement (§ 95 of the Works Constitution Act);
— the employee could be employed elsewhere in the establishment or the company;
— the employee could be employed in another job after retraining which the employer could reasonably be expected to provide;
— the employee could continue to be employed under different contractual terms to which he agrees.

The Works Council is entitled to object to any dismissal which it considers socially unjustifiable on these grounds. If the employer nevertheless dismisses the employee, he must give him a copy of the Works Council's opinion.

Should the employee take the matter to the Labour Court, he has a right to continue to be employed from the expiry of the period of notice until legal proceedings have been concluded. The Court may relieve the employer of this obligation if the application seems unlikely to succeed, or if continued employment would place an unreasonable economic burden on the employer, or if the Works Council's objection was clearly unjustified.

There is special protection against summary dismissal for members of the Works Council and of other legally required representative bodies.

The Works Council can request the dismissal or transfer of employees who habitually break the law or cause trouble in the plant: if the Labour Court finds the request justified, it can be enforced.

The Works Council must also be informed of changes in management staff.

Dismissal for any reason is a risky business without the consent of the Works Council, and this is especially true of the redundancy situation. The employer is required to inform the Works Council of any potential redundancy, and to obtain its agreement in the selection of candidates. Without this, the dismissals can be declared null and void.

Notice. Minimum periods of notice are fixed by law, and differ according to the category of employee (strictly speaking, it depends on whether wages or salaries are paid weekly, monthly etc.). It is however possible for *shorter* periods to be fixed by collective agreement. The periods given below apply to industrial employees: and tend to be widely observed.

manual workers

up to 5 years' service	2 weeks	notice to be
5 years' service	1 month	given for the end
10 years' service	2 months	of the calendar
20 years' service	3 months	month

non-manual workers

up to 5 years' service	6 weeks
5 years' service	3 months
8 years' service	4 months
10 years' service	5 months
12 years' service	6 months

(non-manual employees' entitlements apply also to management staff.)

Limitations. The contract is regarded as suspended in the following cases:

— *illness* (wages must be paid for six weeks; if the worker has been employed for 4 weeks or more, the difference between sickness benefit and net wages for a further six weeks)
— during *military service*
— *pregnancy* and *maternity* (the contract is suspended for six weeks before, and eight weeks after childbirth).

Strikes. A strike does not affect individual contractual relationships, unless the employer retaliates with a lockout, which then constitutes termination of contract. This situation is the subject of some discussion: the legal position will probably be altered in the near future. A recent Court decision permits the employer to terminate contracts only after a lockout following a *wildcat* strike. Thus, in the case of a man locked out during a lawful strike, the contract is by precedent (not yet by Statute) regarded as suspended.

Industrial relations

Legislation

Almost every aspect of relations between employers and employees in Germany is covered by law or collective agreements, and the rights and responsibilities of all parties are clearly defined and generally adhered to. Legislation divides broadly into three types: law protecting the individual; law defining collective rights and obligations; and what can be termed 'co-determinative' law, covering workers' collective participation in management.

Individual law is designed mainly to protect the employee as the economically weaker party. It gives statutory protection to female and young workers; it guarantees paid holidays and limits working hours; it provides for employees to be insured against sickness, old-age, and other 'social risks'; it protects the employee against dismissal at the employer's whim. This type of law also gives the individual the right to a say in the activities of his firm — but through the collective channels provided by co-determinative law. Finally, the individual has a right to belong to a trade union. (It may be noted that he has no explicit right *not* to belong, although this is presumed to be the case.)

The *collective* rights embodied in labour law derive from the individual right to 'form coalitions' for the purpose of negotiating terms and conditions of employment. The Collective Agreements Act reinforces the collective principle by giving authority to conclude agreements only to trade unions and employers and employers' associations, and this has inevitably led to high levels of organisation on both sides of the negotiating table. The main features of conditions of employment are therefore regulated in national or regional bargaining, although a few very large companies — e.g. Volkswagenwerk — enter into company agreements with the union. The law to some extent determines what can be agreed by whom at what level, but in general it recognises the autonomy of the bargaining parties. While the State may, for example, offer its services as mediator following a breakdown in collective negotiations, it cannot normally impose compulsory conciliation or arbitration — for which the bargaining partners have their own agreed procedures.

Co-determinative law takes several forms. On the one hand it gives the employees a collective right to representation along with shareholders' representatives on the Boards of a company. On the other it gives them the right to be represented on a Works Council — with some important rights of co-decision — which is distinct from trade union representation. These rights are embodied in the Co-determination Act 1951 (for the iron and steel industry) and the Works Constitution Act 1972 for other sectors of the economy. The Works Council cannot be compared with a British shop stewards' committee. In the plant, the function of trade unions is to watch over the implementation of collective agreements, which have been concluded at regional or national level. The 1972 Act has increased their influence in matters affecting the Works Council; but the Works Council remains a body for employee representation within the plant irrespective of union membership, and has a primary duty of loyalty to the enterprise. The Works Council now has some rights of co-decision on the question of pay: but the plant trade union representatives do not. 'Plant bargaining' is undoubtedly increasing in Germany, but its limits are strictly defined by law and collective agreement.

The State, therefore has created a framework of law within which the collective bargaining partners operate a largely voluntary system of industrial relations. Labour courts exist for those seeking redress for any breach of legal requirements, but the courts have practically no rights of initiation of proceedings by the State in, for example, industrial disputes, except in certain circumstances under the Emergency Powers Act.

This system depends on the acceptance by both sides of industry of the economic and political status quo. The trade unions' attitude of co-operation has the inevitable corollary of co-responsibility, which has found expression in the various laws giving employees rights of co-determination. By a continuing tradition of consensus politics, the German worker has achieved the highest degree of influence on the control and management of industry in Europe. It has also contributed to a world-record of industrial relations stability. But it is probably too facile to attribute this stability solely to such institutional arrangements and to such co-operative philosophies. High levels of employment, strong growth rates and the containment of inflation have contributed just as much to non-militancy. There is evidence that, when this favourable situation falters, as many wild-cat strikes can be expected in Germany as in any other country.

Trade unions

Roughly ⅓ of the working population belong to trade unions. The overwhelming majority — six and à half million — are members of the 16 industry-wide unions which form the DGB (Deutscher Gewerkschaftsbund/German Confederation of Trade Unions). These unions are open to manual and staff workers, and public employees, they have no political or religious affiliation, although the DGB is broadly social-democrat, and has supplied a number of the SPD front bench. The percentage of organised workers in each industrial sector varies widely:

— Commerce, Banking & Insurance Union	4%
— Public Services and Transport Union	25%
— Mining and Energy Union	85%
— Engineering (IG Metall)	53%

IG Metall is numerically the strongest union, with almost two and a quarter million members.

The member unions of the DGB normally negotiate terms and conditions for their own sector: the DGB does negotiate as a body in some circumstances. The DGB favours co-operation and co-responsibility in a free enterprise economy, but its aims include the nationalisation of key industries. It also seeks a voice in overall national economic planning, and did in fact join with industrialists in the SPD Government's 'concerted action'. One of the DGB's main policies is considerably increased co-determination in industry, and it lobbied strongly for 50% worker representation on company Supervisory Boards during the debate which led up to the passage of the recent Works Constitution Act. (This is also part of the SPD's programme, which was dropped as a condition of the coalition with the Free Democrats. It may well reappear if the SPD ever receives an overall majority.)

Not all unions belong to the DGB, nor are they all organised on an industry-wide basis. The DAG (Deutsche Angestellten-Gewerkschaft/German Staffworkers' Union) is restricted to staff-workers, and draws its membership of 480,000 from all branches of industry and commerce. The DBB (Deutscher Beamtenbund/German Federation of Civil Servants) has some 700,000 members. Despite their relatively small memberships, these two unions have considerable influence. There is additionally a very small white-collar federation with Christian-nationalist leanings, the CGB. It is estimated that some 23.5% of all staff employees belong to trade unions.

There have so far been few signs of management unionism; paternalist traditions have died slowly in Germany, and unions in general still suffer from a certain stigma. Nevertheless, it is interesting to note that a management union called the Union der leitenden Angestellten (UlA) has been formed, and has a membership of about 30,000. As yet it has no collective bargaining influence.

Employers' associations

Employers are organised in regional associations, according to branch of industry, which form federations at national level — perhaps the best known of these is Gesamtmetall for the engineering industry. The regional associations also combine at Land level to form general employers' federations, which, together with the national branch federations, form the BDA (Bundesverband der deutschen Arbeit-geberverbände/Confederation of German Employers' Federations). About 80% of employers are members of the 44 branch federations and the 14 Land federations. The employers' association covering the iron and steel industries does not belong to the BDA because of the special arrangements for co-determination which exist in that sector. The BDA is exclusively an employers' confederation: its equivalent trade association is the BDI (Bundesverband der deutschen Industrie/Confederation of German Industry).

Collective bargaining

Collective agreements can be conducted only by individual employers, employers' associations and trade unions or trade union confederations. In the main they are agreed between the bargaining partners in a particular branch of industry, at national or regional level. (In engineering, for example, agreements are concluded regionally but all at the same time, and with central co-ordination both of the terms, and of the industrial action which may be undertaken.) They can also be concluded by an individual employer and a union: or by the national partners in respect of an individual firm.

The object is to agree minimum standard terms and conditions of employment. In many cases, conditions are agreed in a framework or model agreement (Mantel- or Rahmentarifvertrag), with rates of pay being agreed in separate agreements of shorter duration — usually between one and two years. The kind of condition agreed in the framework agreement may be not only holidays, hours of work, etc., but also general grading structures for the wages and salaries which are to be agreed in the agreements of shorter duration. In addition, there may be special agreements on specific subjects — introduction of shorter working hours phased over several years, for example, or protection of jobs during rationalisation measures.

One of the most important features of a collective agreement is the obligation to keep the industrial peace. Neither party may engage in activity in support of new claims while the agreement covering that particular area is still in force.

The standard minimum conditions laid down by collective agreements automatically bind both parties to the individual contract of employment, if they are members of the relevant association or union. The agreement cannot, however, declare the conditions to be maximum: and more favourable conditions can be domestically agreed,

either

(a) in the individual contract of employment

or

(b) by Works Agreement (between the Works Council and the employer). Only if the collective agreement expressly permits this can wages and standard conditions be improved in this way. Otherwise works agreements cannot be made on subjects regulated by collective agreement. There are, however, some subjects which are left open, including some with influence on payment systems.

Maximum standard conditions cannot be agreed for two reasons. Firstly because collective agreements can in principle provide for conditions less favourable than certain legal provisions. In a situation where the provisions of, say, an agreement, a law, or a works regulation could all apply, the employee is entitled to be treated according to the most favourable provision of the three which could apply. Secondly because, as minima for a wide range of workers, they do not permit individual performance or exceptional circumstances to be taken into account. 'Efficiency bonuses' and, latterly,, merit-rating bonuses, play a significant role in German payment systems.

Wage agreements

National or regional wage agreements usually fix the standard rate for general categories of employees. The number of grades varies according to region and sector, and may lie between 5 and 12. These may take into account qualifications and physical requirements, responsibility and perhaps particular items such as dirty work etc. In some cases job grading structures are fairly sophisticated, involving detailed examples of jobs of greater or lesser difficulty, delicate gradations of a 'sense of responsibility' and so on.

Several techniques govern the relationship of agreed standard minimum rates, and their increases, to domestic rates and earnings levels: and most of these will be familiar from British experience. Bonuses may be consolidated into new rates, for example, if the bonus was initially granted as a reflection of inadequate standard rates. Similarly, the national agreement may incorporate clauses which maintain the differential between standard and domestic rates. The 'effective earnings clause' *(Effektivklausel)* guarantees a general increase, in that higher earnings cannot be offset against the new standard rates. Wage drift, in the sense of the differential between agreed minima and earnings, lies between 5% and 30% in Germany according to sector and region.

Extension of the collective agreement. The collective agreement normally applies to members of the bodies which conclude it. (An employer who is a member of the employers' association is always so bound). If, however,

(a) the employers party to the agreement employ at least 50% of the workers in the sector; and

(b) it appears to be in the public interest, the terms of the agreement may be extended by the Minister of Labour to cover the entire sector. This is frequent in the building trades.

Breakdown in negotiations. If negotiations break down, the bargaining partners proceed to conciliation according to a procedure voluntarily agreed between them. There is neither compulsory conciliation nor compulsory arbitration in Germany, although two Land constitutions still contain the necessary legislation. The parties are not obliged to accept the recommendations of the neutral mediator, who has to be acceptable to both sides. If conciliation is fruitless, the way is open for industrial action: indeed, this is widely held to be the only circumstance in which a strike is lawful. It is indicative of union attitudes that the constitutions of most unions require a two-thirds majority vote — of the whole membership — to initiate industrial action. Even then, strike pay may be withheld on the decision of the union's governing authorities. Official lawful strikes have become slightly more frequent in recent years; and employers too have become more militant. In a recent conflict in the engineering industry in Baden-Württemberg, employers locked out three non-striking workers for every one striker. As this also affected non-unionists, the legal position is unclear, but this kind of action seems unlikely to become a regular feature of German industrial relations.

Strikes

Wildcat strikes are illegal, unless they are subsequently recognised by the union; political strikes are also not permitted. In these cases, strikers may be liable for losses incurred by the employer — compensation of 500,000 Deutschmarks was recently awarded against half a dozen individuals. Equally, the employer is obliged to pay those employees who are willing to work during a lockout. This willingness, however, is often difficult to prove. The obligation to pay wages is suspended during a strike: and similarly when workers are laid off as a result of a strike in another company. The obligation continues when the same situation results from another employer's lockout.

Conditions of employment

Remuneration

The standard rates fixed by collective agreements apply to the three most widespread payment systems in Germany:

- time work
- piecework (with a guaranteed earnings level corresponding at least to the standard time rate) — piecework is not allowed by law as a form of payment for juvenile workers on the grounds that it imposes strain
- the premium system, i.e. fixed basic plus output-related bonus.

Wage payment systems are very much subject to analytical measurement and evaluation techniques, starting with Bedaux. In the height of the Depression, a number of techniques were agreed which became known as REFA: at present this system is somewhat in decline, but it has lasted well and indicates that the principles of analytical evaluation are commonly accepted. The basic significance of this is that individual or plant negotiations revolve around the price rather than the time. The Works Council now has considerable influence in this area, and the Works Constitution Act goes as far as mentioning money factors as the subject for domestic co-decision.

On top of the basic elements of payment a number of bonuses are common, ranging from productivity bonuses to bonuses reflecting individual skills or qualifications, or even punctuality and personal sense of responsibility. As mentioned elsewhere, there is considerable interest in the principle of merit-rating.

Special bonuses, paid on a once-for-all basis, may be agreed in national, regional or domestic bargaining, or as part of the individual contract. If these are paid repeatedly, they automatically become part of the legal wage (where an 'ex gratia' bonus is company policy, it too becomes part of the legal wage if it is paid for three years without qualification).

Wages

According to E.E.C. statistics, real hourly wages (as adjusted by movements in the consumer price index) rose by 41% between 1964 and 1971. The rate of increase has flattened out in the last few years, as inflation has caught up, and there is evidence that it dropped from around 6.5% in 1969/70 to 3% in 1970/71. Nevertheless, German workers are among the highest paid in Europe. Earnings, on average, are low in Bavaria, Schleswig-Holstein and the Saar (see Appendix (iii), p.111); and, despite equal pay provisions, females earn on average 70-75% of men's earnings. (For sector differentials, see Appendix (ii), p.110.)

Working hours

The legal maximum normal working hours are 48 per week, 8 per day. Collective agreements have reduced this, so that for industry the 40-hour week is usual, and the vast majority of employees work a five-day week.

Overtime

Average hours worked in the manufacturing industries were

	1969	*1970*	*1971*	
April	44.0	44.1	42.9	
October	44.2	44.0	43.3	(E.E.C. statistics)

Hours tend to be higher in shipbuilding (around 47) and lower in chemicals and textiles. By region, there is no wide spread; West Berlin, however, shows below-average hours worked.

Overtime is calculated, for payment purposes, on daily working hours and weekly hours in the south (Bavaria, Hessen etc.). Rates lie between 25% and 50% of the basic wage, e.g. the North-Rhine/Westphalia engineering agreement, calculated on daily hours, fixes overtime for the first two hours at time and a quarter and the third and subsequent hours at time and a half. (NB: basic wage = basic rate + regular allowances and bonuses.) The textile industry pays time and a third for the third and subsequent hours.

Shiftwork and nightwork supplements

Provisions for shiftwork and nightwork vary considerably, by region and sector. In general, no payment is made for day-shift working; nightshift, and regular nightwork is paid at between 10% and 25% above basic wage. Exceptional nightwork is paid at time and a half.

Annual holidays and public holidays

Legally-required minimum paid holidays are 15 days after six months' service, and 18 days at age 35 and above. These are usually increased by collective agreement and may vary by sector and seniority between 18 and 26 days. Holidays are paid at average hourly earnings (over a 13-week reference period). Additional bonuses may be paid by collective agreement or individual agreement.

Public holidays are 10-13 by sector and region. In the latter case, the dominating religion decides when holidays are not general throughout the country.

Religious holidays subject to regional variation are in square brackets in the following list:

New Year's Day
[Epiphany]
Easter Monday
May Day
Ascension Day
Whit Monday
[Corpus Christi]
[Assumption Day]
[All Saints]
Christmas Day
Boxing Day
Day of German Unity (17th June)
Day of Prayer and Repentance (November)

Public holidays are paid at average earnings, but not if they fall on a Sunday or a Saturday which is not normally worked. Some public holidays require the following Saturday to be worked in compensation.

Work on normally non-worked Saturdays is paid at overtime rates; Sunday working at time and a half. Work on public holidays is paid with a bonus of 100-150%.

Social security

Social security provisions are based on the insurance principle usual in Europe.

Pensions (covering disability, retirement, death). The basic system, as required by law, covers manual and staff employees. It is, however, administered by regional institutions for the former (Krankenkasse or Ersatzkasse) and a national institution for the latter.

The contributions are:

Employer 8.5%
Employee 8.5%   of earnings

There may be additional pension schemes arranged by collective agreement (there is one covering the building trades) or by company practice. There may be:

(a) private self-administered funds
(b) group insurance schemes
(c) tax-free unfunded schemes ('Retirement Benefit Pledge')

The Government is planning to fill various gaps in the German pension system — particularly loss of rights when changing jobs, and, in case (c), complete loss of benefit if the company goes bankrupt.

Accident insurance. This covers industrial injuries and diseases, and provides for medical care, and where necessary re-training. It will also meet employers' liability compensation. Contributions are entirely from the employer, the price of cover varying in accordance with familiar insurance principles (ranging from 1%-11% of the wage bill). The fund is run by the Industrial Accident Insurance Institute or occupationally structured 'Berufsgenossenschaften'.

Health insurance. This is administered by a variety of institutions — local (Ortskrankenkassen), company (Betriebskrankenkassen), occupational (Innungskrankenkassen), free (Ersatszkassen) etc. Contributions, paid 50:50 by employer and employee, are between 7% and 9% of earnings.

Unemployment insurance. This is administered by the State. Contributions, again divided equally between employer and employee, are about 1.3% of wages and salaries up to 1,900 DM per month.

Total labour cost — E.E.C. breakdown for 1969

Manual workers	%
1. Direct wages and regular bonuses	69.19
2. Other bonuses and *ex gratia* payments	2.88
3. Payment for days not worked (holidays etc.)	10.31
4. Employer's social security contributions	
— sickness, disability, maternity, retirement, unemployment	11.02
— industrial accidents and diseases	1.81
— family allowances (financed by the State)	—
— other legal contributions	0.02
TOTAL, statutory contributions	12.84
— company or sector insurance schemes	0.02
— supplementary retirement pensions	1.39
— contractual or voluntary wage and salary guarantee	0.05
— supplementary unemployment insurance	—
— contractual supplementary family allowances	0.25
— other contractual and voluntary payments	0.05
TOTAL, contractual and voluntary payments	1.76
TOTAL, employer contributions to social security	14.61
5. Payments in kind	0.67
6. Other payments of social nature	1.38
7. Training costs	0.96
8. Social taxes	—
TOTAL LABOUR COST	100.00

Source:
Social Statistics Labour Cost (Preliminary results) 1969 — Published 1971 by the Statistical Office of the European Communities.

Total labour cost — E.E.C. breakdown for 1969

Staff employees	%
1. Direct wages and regular bonuses	72.51
2. Other bonuses and *ex gratia* payments	—
3. Payments for days not worked (holidays etc.)	9.91
4. Employer's social security contributions	
— sickness, disability, maternity, retirement, unemployment	8.33
— industrial accidents and diseases	1.00
— family allowances (financed by the State)	—
— other legal contributions	0.02
TOTAL, statutory contributions	9.34
— company or sector insurance schemes	0.18
— supplementary retirement pensions	4.76
— contractual or voluntary wage and salary guarantee	0.06
— supplementary unemployment insurance	—
— contractual supplementary family allowances	0.32
— other contractual and voluntary payments	0.06
TOTAL, contractual and voluntary payments	5.38
TOTAL, employer contributions to social security	14.72
5. Payments in kind	0.52
6. Other payments of social nature	1.34
7. Training costs	1.00
8. Social taxes	—
TOTAL LABOUR COST	100.00

Employee representation

Germany has a long tradition — fifty years — of employee representation through Works Councils. The rights of these bodies have recently been considerably extended such that they have powers of co-decision in management proposals on a number of matters. Since the war, employees — and to some extent through trade unions — have also had representation on company Boards. This is facilitated by the German system of company law, and is important because the system in increasingly finding favour in other E.E.C. countries. The system is also recommended for the proposed European company statute.

German companies have a two-tier Board structure: a Supervisory Board (Aufsichtsrat) which appoints, and supervises the activities of, a Management Board (Vorstand), which is responsible for the day-to-day running of the company. Originally, the Supervisory Board represented, and was elected by, the shareholders. Since its main function is supervisory, however, it was held to be reasonable that it should also represent other interests in the company. There are now two systems in operation — one applying to companies in the mining, iron and steel sector, and the other applying to all joint stock companies with more than 500 employees and all limited liability companies.

Co-determination in the Mining, Iron and Steel Sector

Supervisory Boards in this sector have at least eleven members — up to 21 in large companies. The minimum requirements are as follows:

> *Shareholders' representatives*
> 4 members + 1 additional member
> *Workers' representatives*
> 4 members — of whom 1 manual and 1 staff worker — + 1 additional member
> (up to 2 workers' members — or, in larger Boards, more — can be workers from outside the company — for example, from the trade union)
> *plus* 1 neutral member

(The 'additional members' for each side cannot have a large financial interest in the firm, nor can they belong to it as employer or employee, nor be a representative of a trade union or an employers' association.)

In this sector, when the Supervisory Board appoints the Management Board, it is required to appoint additionally a 'Labour Director'. He cannot be either appointed or dismissed without the agreement of the majority of workers' representatives. In practice, the Labour Director is usually appointed on the nomination of the trade unions. His responsibilities are specifically personnel and industrial relations, but his vote counts equally in the deliberations of the Management Board.

Representation on the Boards of other companies

The Supervisory Board has 3-21 members — the figure must be divisible by 3. Here, shareholders' representatives have ⅔ of the seats, and the workers ⅓. In this case also, there is no special requirement on the composition of the Management Board.

In all cases, members of the Supervisory Board have a primary duty to the interests of the company rather than their sectional interests: the personal financial liability is the same for all Supervisory Board members.

The Works Council (Betriebsrat)

The law currently in force under which Works Councils must be set up is the *Works Constitution Act,* which came into effect at the beginning of 1972, and much extended the provisions of the previous Act of 1952. This law is extremely comprehensive and, in addition to its provisions relating to the Works Council, it sets up a Youth Committee; increases trade union access to the plant; and defines a number of rights for individual employees.

A Works Council must be set up in all establishments with 5 or more employees, although in practice by no means all such companies have Works Councils. For multi-plant companies, a Central Works Council is required: in the case of a large concern, the Central Works Councils may decide to form, in addition, a Concern Works Council.

The Works Council has 1-31 members according to the number of employees in firms employing up to 9000; beyond this, 2 more members are elected for every further 3000 employees. There are special rules by which a roughly proportional representation of manual and staff is achieved: they are elected separately, and all members are elected for three years.

The Works Council has a basic duty, in co-operation with the trade unions and employers' associations represented in the plant, to monitor the domestic implementation of collective agreements. It also has a fiduciary duty to the company, and employer and Works Council may not indulge in acts of industrial warfare as a result.

The Works Council has a number of important rights of co-determination, consultation and information.

Co-determination

Rights of co-determination are subject to the qualification that they are not applicable to questions already fixed by law or collective agreement. In cases of disagreement, a conciliation committee can make a binding decision at the request of either side. This conciliation committee consists of representatives of Works Council and employer, with a neutral chairman from outside the company. The Works Council has such co-determination rights on matters involving:

- the smooth running of the plant, and employees' conduct
- arrangement of daily working time, breaks, distribution over the week of working hours
- temporary variations in working time (e.g. short-time)
- place, time and manner of wage payment
- holiday schedule planning
- regulations on matters affecting safety and health
- plant welfare amenities
- company housing allocation
- introduction and application of equipment used for surveillance of employees' conduct or productivity
- matters relating to domestic payment systems, including the introduction of new systems
- determination of piece rates and premium rates; and of performance-related rates, including money factors
- principles for suggestion schemes

Plant agreements can be made on

a) additional measures for the prevention of industrial accidents and health hazards
b) welfare institutions limited to the plant
c) measures for promoting employees' capital formation

Consultation and co-determination

- Recruitment, grading, regrading and transfers
  (advance information is required. In individual cases, as
  noted under *Contracts,* the Works Council's objection may
  be enforced by the Labour Court.)
- Dismissals (see *Contracts).*
- Overall personnel and manpower planning (advance information
  and consultation.)
- Personal files (general principles for personal assessment need
  Works Council assent.)
- Criteria for selection in redundancy, transfer etc. situations
  (in cases of disagreement, the conciliation committee may
  issue a binding decision.)

Information and consultation

The Works Council must be informed and consulted on major
changes, including plant closure, or merger, changes of organisation,
product, plant. Where there is disagreement, the Act provides only
for *mediation* by the local employment office or the conciliation
committee, but no binding decision can be made. If however the
change will involve major personnel changes, the conciliation committee can enforce the Works Council's request for a 'social plan'
to be set up.

Vocational training is also subject to the Works Council's right
of co-determination. Disagreement on plant vocational training
measures can be resolved by the conciliation committee's binding
decision. The Works Council can insist on the appointment of a
training officer and, if he lacks the relevant qualifications and
qualities, can apply for him to be dismissed. In this case, the
ultimate decision lies with the Labour Court.

A *Youth Committee* is required in plants with at least 5 workers
under 18. The Committee has 1-9 members under the age of 24.
Their function is to represent the interests of young workers: one
of their number attends all Works Council meetings — the whole
Committee, if the matter under discussion primarily affects young
workers. If a decision of the Works Council is held to be against the
interests of young employees, the Youth Committee can suspend
that decision for one week.

An *Economic Committee* is appointed by the Works Council in plants with more than 100 employees. The Committee has a right of information on: the economic and financial situation, production and sales, investment programme, rationalisation plans and other information affecting employee interests.

Safety Officers employed by the firm now join the employer in meetings with the Works Council at least once a month.

2. Italy

Recruitment

Employees are recruited through the national Employment Service. Employers must apply to the local office covering the place of employment, specifying numbers and skills or qualifications required; and normally they must accept the people they are sent, with the following exceptions:

- no application is needed for management personnel, or for close relatives
- for certain professions, and for particular skills, an employer may name the worker he wishes to employ
- an employer is not obliged to accept a worker who has been dismissed for 'just cause' (see *Dismissals*) but workers who are unemployed as a result of redundancy have priority
- no application is necessary in cases where employees are being transferred from one plant to another belonging to the same firm.

In emergencies, an employer may take on workers without going through the employment office, but must justify this if their employment lasts more than 3 days.

All new engagements must be reported to the relevant public (police) authority within five days; and all changes in the labour force must be similarly reported in the first 5 days of each month.

It should be noted that establishments employing more than 35 workers must reserve 15% of jobs for certain categories; of that 15%, 25% for war invalids; 15% for invalids from the civil war or from industrial accidents and their survivors and civil invalids; and 5% for deaf and dumb workers. The employer in such cases must report on the situation twice a year to the local Employment Office. Additionally, there are requirements concerning the employment of blind workers; and firms employing more than

50 workers must keep 10% of places open to refugees from former Italian colonial possessions, and former territory.

Foreign workers require an entry visa obtainable from the local Italian consular representation, before entry. Applications must be supported by a request from the Italian employer, who is himself obliged to make a detailed request to the local Employment Office. If the request is suitably phrased, the Employment Office will be in a position to make a declaration that no nationals are available or qualified to fill the job, and this may speed up the administrative process. The worker is therefore required to have a valid entry permit before entry, and then a residence permit dependent on a work permit. For E.E.C. nationals, however, only a residence permit is required for entry, a passport or identity card suffices, and the public authority (e.g. police) will issue a permit 'for citizens of an E.E.C. member State' on production of a statement of appointment or engagement by the employer. This is valid for 5 years and renewable.

Foreigners working in Italy who are paid by a firm operating in another country do not normally require a permit if they are there for less than a month if, in general terms, they are highly specialised and are, for example, negotiating on behalf of their firm, or acting as, for example, commercial traveller.

In all cases, employers in Italy are obliged to inform the public authorities within 24 hours of engaging or dismissing foreign (or Stateless) employees.

Contract of employment

The form. A contract of service comes into existence on the engagement of executives and higher managers; staff employees; and manual workers (foremen and supervisors are generally considered as a further, intermediate category). A *written* letter of engagement is obligatory only for staff employees, but is usual in all cases, especially where the content is laid down by collective agreement.

Content. The essential contents are:

   — the place of work
   — the date of commencement
   — the grade or professional status
   — the terms of remuneration
   — where applicable, the length of any probationary period.

Duration. The contract of employment is in principle of indefinite duration. Fixed-term contracts are only valid in the written form, and are permitted only in the following cases:

— where the job is seasonal (but only where it is so defined by decree)
— where the employee is replacing employees whose jobs the employer is obliged to hold open (e.g. because of military service, pregnancy etc.)
— where the employee is hired in respect of a specific job or service to be completed or rendered within a specified period and the job or service is of an exceptional nature
— where a project has to be carried out in successive stages, each requiring a different kind of labour (such as certain types of site construction: this provision would not apply to normal industrial production)
— for artistes and technical personnel in entertainment.

Employees on a fixed-term contract must be treated in every respect like those on open-ended contracts: effectively the sole difference lies in the absence of provisions for notice of termination.

Probationary periods or contracts must be defined in writing. They are frequently laid down in collective agreements and therefore differ according to the professional status of the employee. They may be neither prolonged nor renewed; and may be terminated by either party at any time, without notice or payment in lieu.

Labour documents. To qualify for engagement, staff and manual employees must by law possess a valid 'labour card' issued by the Ministry of Labour and Social Security, which must be presented on engagement. Other documents may also require to be presented in accordance with collective agreements. These may include social security card, health insurance card (INAM), statement of civil status (to qualify for family allowances), identity card etc.

Medical inspection. The law requires certain categories of workers to undergo medical examination before engagement. This applies to employees in foodstuffs, those in industrial occupations which expose them to toxic or infection-carrying substances, and in jobs which carry obligatory insurance against asbestosis and silicosis; also employees under 18 and apprentices.

Most collective agreements provide for the employer to be able to require medical inspection before engagement, even where no legal obligation exists.

Termination of contract — dismissal and redundancy

There are two basic grounds for dismissal.

(a) *'Just cause'* (Giusta causa) is defined — in the Civil Code — as one which 'does not permit the — even provisional — continuance of the contractual relationship', with particular reference to loss of good faith and confidence essential in a contract of service. 'Just cause' is grounds for summary dismissal without notice, payment in lieu or severance pay.

(b) *'Justifiable reason'* relates to a failure to observe a term of the contract, or reasons arising from changes in production, work organisation and the employee's normal job.

The grounds of 'justifiable reason' therefore can be invoked both for individual and collective dismissals. In the latter case, the redundancy situation itself must be justifiable. The onus of proof falls here on the employer: and if within one year jobs become available for which the redundant workers' skills are adequate, they must be given priority.

Dismissal must be notified in writing, and the dismissed employee has a right, within a week from notification, to request a written statement of the employer's reasons — which must be supplied within 5 days of the request. No action may be taken if the question is progressed through the disputes procedure (as agreed between the trade unions and the employers association) or where, if the question is not resolved at that level, subsequent reference is made to a Labour Court. If the dismissal is held by the Court to be invalid by default of just cause or justified reason, the employee must be reinstated; in addition he is to receive an indemnity of five months' pay and normal, full remuneration as from the date of the judgment.

If a dismissal is found to have been occasioned by reason of political or religious conviction, membership of a trade union or participation in union activities, it will be declared null and void.

NB. Members of the Commissione Interna are entitled to further protection from dismissal.

Redundancy situations must be notified in advance to trade unions and employees' representatives, with whom a meeting must be held to discuss possible alternatives.

All provisions relating to termination of contract cover all employees — manual and staff as well as professional and managerial employees.

Notice. Notice of dismissal or termination is required in every case except where the contract is a fixed-term one, or when the worker is dismissed summarily. If notice is not given, payment in lieu for the contractual period of notice must be given. (This also applies when the employee terminates his contract and must indemnify his employer.) For all purposes, the contractual relationship lasts until the end of the period of notice. If payment in lieu is made, the period to which the indemnity corresponds is deemed to be included in the period of contractual relationship if the decision to pay in lieu is made unilaterally by the employer. If an indemnity is paid by mutual agreement, the contract terminates at the date of notification.

Periods of notice are laid down by law (for staff employees) and collective agreement; or otherwise by custom and practice:

manual workers	6 days (48 hours) − 15 days (120 hours) (according to sector and seniority)
foremen and supervisors	1 month − 1½ months (according to sector and seniority)
staff employees	1 month − 4 months (legal minimum − 15 days)
management	5 months − 12 months

Dismissal indemnity − the 'seniority bonus'. Severance pay fixed in accordance with length of service has been legally required for staff employees since the 20s, but nowadays by custom and practice this 'seniority bonus' is applied to *all* employees dismissed, from executive to manual. Furthermore, it is now paid in all circumstances − even in cases of summary dismissal where the employee is not entitled to notice.

The Civil Code requires that the bonus take into account
a) years of service with the same firm, and
b) the *total* remuneration (including fringe benefits, family allowances etc) which the employee was last receiving.

At present the rates are:

manual workers	6 days (= in practice 40 hours) pay for the first and second years of service; plus 26 days (= in practice 106 hours) for the tenth and subsequent years of service
foremen and supervisors	rates vary, but are equal to those applying to staff employees for years of service completed after 1969

staff employees	1 month's pay per year of service
management	1 month's salary for each of the first ten years' service; thereafter, 1½ months' salary for year of service. (Years of service acquired in other grades are included and uniformly treated.)

The bonus is also paid to dependants in the case of an employee's death, in addition to payment in lieu of the notice he would have received. (This is *not* limited to death arising from industrial accident.)

Redundancy payment. For 180 days, employees dismissed in a redundancy situation are paid a sum equivalent to ⅔ of the pay which they were last receiving.

Limitations. In certain circumstances the contract cannot be terminated but is regarded as suspended:

— *illness* (over a period of 6 − 12 months)
— *industrial accident or sickness* (until a certificate of recovery has been issued)
— *maternity* a woman may not be dismissed during pregnancy and for one year after live childbirth except for 'just cause', factory closedown, end of fixed-term contract or failure to observe a main term of the contract. In the last three months of pregnancy and for the first three months after live childbirth a woman may not be dismissed for any reason whatever.
— *marriage* (women may not be dismissed in the period from the publication of the banns until the ceremony and for one year thereafter, except for 'just cause', factory closure, end of fixed-term contract or failure to observe a main term of the contract.
— *military service* (the contract is regarded as suspended, but no years of service accrue to the employee)

In all these cases, there can be *no dismissal within three months* of recommencing work.

Strikes. The contract of employment is not affected by lawful strikes: the complementary obligations of carrying out work and paying wages are regarded as suspended only. In all other respects the contractual relationship is uninterrupted.

Lockouts. The obligation to pay wages is not suspended during a lockout.

Industrial relations

Italy's industrial relations are notorious for their enormously high levels of days lost through strikes, the overtly political nature of strikes, and the way in which strikes appear to break out *ad libendum* through all sectors of the economy. The Italian worker's reputation in this respect even surpasses the international reputation of his British counterpart, except that in the case of the former, a great deal is written off to the account of Italy's political instability. In fact, the instability goes deeper than politics alone. Since the war, and in particular in the last 10-15 years, Italy has undergone vast industrial expansion. The switch from agricultural to industrial employment has been rapid, and has brought a large, mainly unskilled, working population into industrial cities where they have no roots. Simultaneously, rapid industrial reorganisation has occurred: the existing high percentage of very small firms, and low number of very large firms is not adequate to the demands of a modern industrial state; and the resultant rationalisation − or fear of rationalisation − has left an already insecure labour force of new-comers in unskilled and frequently boring jobs feeling even more unsafe. A country at this stage of industrialisation is highly susceptible to economic booms and recessions, which cannot be centrally controlled. To some observers, in fact, this might be a classic Marxist situation, ripe for revolution. It is perhaps ironic that the flux in the social situation in Italy is a result of the country's basic economic strength and potential.

Flux and change have also characterised the industrial relations situation. The unions are predominantly political in nature, their members − and equally a majority of non-members − also have a mainly political outlook. With this in mind, it is perhaps not surprising, in the context, that they have appeared to be negotiating with Governments rather than employers − indeed they are, and with considerable success. Their interests are bound to include overall employment policies, especially as regards underdeveloped regions; it is inevitable, with such rapid developments over the past decade, that they are as concerned with basic political attitudes to work as they are with negotiating wages − and strong shopfloor movements, both inside and outside of union membership, are equally concerned with the question of whether unions should negotiate such wages on their behalf, or whether the process should be more direct (the slogan being 'We are the trade union'). The result is militancy at all levels in all directions. The overall situation is very unclear.

Italy's industrial relations are now suffering from a bald conflict between an obviously inadequate formal system, which has been built up since the war, and a lively, shopfloor based informal system which has not yet fully decided whether its activities complement or replace those of the official, national unions. The outcome is unpredictable, but it is possible that the ultimate synthesis will provide a dynamic — and expensive — industrial relations system of a more representative nature.

For the reasons outlined above, it is difficult to quantify what is going on: statistics cannot reflect it. It will be possible, however, to describe the minimum norms laid down within the ambit of the formal system by law and collective agreements, and to add qualification in terms of trends which have recently been in evidence.

Authorities and collective representation

The State

Through the Ministry of Labour and Social Security, the State takes on the protection of workers in respect of legal requirements; in particular, the Ministry deals with

- vocational training
- employment matters (see *Contracts*)
- regulation of industrial relations (mediation in major disputes, including those arising from collective agreements)
- social security, and the conduct of the institutions involved
- statistics

The Ministry operates through (i) regional and provincial employment offices and (ii) the Labour Inspectorate, who have the right of access to all plants.

Trade unions

About 50% of Italy's working population — some 10 million — are organised in the member unions of several large confederations, each of which represents a different political orientation. These are:

CGIL   (Confederazione Generale Italiana del Lavoro/Italian General Confederation of Labour): CGIL has about 4 million members; its politics are Communist/Socialist.

CISL   (Confederazione Italiana Sindicati Lavoratori/Italian Confederation of Labour Unions) with about 3 million members. CISL's politics are Christian-Democrat.

UIL   (Unione Italiana del Lavoro/Italian Labour Union)
          representing some 800,000-1 million members of
          socialist, social-democrat and republican orientation.
CISNAL   (Confederazione Italiana Sindicati Nazionali Lavoratori/
          Italian Confederation of National Labour Unions), and
CISAL   (Confederazione Italiana Sindicati Autonomi Lavoratori/
          Italian Confederation of Autonomous Labour Unions)
          are both relatively small confederations.

CGIL, CISL and UIL were originally one very large confederation,
but split in the late 40s for political reasons. They have now declared
that they will merge in 1973 and if this happens, the resulting body
will be unprecedentedly powerful. Each of the confederations consists of unions covering individual branches of industry. The resulting
disparate situation has not mattered too much while the formal
collective bargaining structure was effective. With the growth of the
shopfloor movement, and what might be termed 'semi-formal'
plant bargaining, which has taken little account of union membership or non-membership, a new, strong central union situation has
become desirable; and the proposed merger may well produce
this. But problems have already arisen. The unions which cover
engineering in the various confederations have already started to co-
operate (the engineering negotiations occupy a leading position for
the rest of industry), and considerable tensions between them and
their confederations have arisen. The autumn of 1972 saw the
announcement of a new split between the confederations, and the
merger may now be indefinitely postponed.

A management staff confederation, CIDA (Confederazione Italiana
Dirigenti di Azienda/Italian Contederation of Management Staff)
also exists, but has so far not allied itself either with the employers'
or the unions' interests.

Employers' associations

The State has very large holdings in Italian industry, ranging from
wholly-owned enterprises, such as Alitalia, to minority holdings in
private firms. One reason for this is the necessity, as already mentioned, of transforming the structure of Italian industry to meet the
requirements of a post-war industrial State: and the State-holding
companies play a large part in rationalisation and re-structuring. In
some ways they can be regarded as the former UK Industrial Re-
organisation Corporation writ very large indeed. The fact of these
large organisations helps explain why any form of industrial action
in Italy is a move against the Government directly — in this way, the
Government is the employer of a large proportion of the working
population.

By law, State-owned enterprises are not permitted to make common cause with employers in the private sector for the purposes of collective bargaining (although trade associations for both sectors co-operate with each other). Employers are therefore organised separately:
  State-owned, and semi-public holdings are covered by:
  — INTERSIND for companies controlled by IRI, the State re-organisation corporation,
  — ASAP for firms involved with ENI (Ente Nazionali Idrocarburi) which co-ordinates State involvement in the petrochemical industry.

Private industry is represented by the Confindustria (Confederazione Generale dell Industria Italiana/General Confederation of Italian industry). In the past, Confindustria's structure has taken the form of a relatively loose co-ordination of autonomous — and frequently regional — associations for individual sectors. For example, the most important associations for the private engineering sector are, not surprisingly, in Turin and Milan. Recently, however, Confindustria has been rationalising and strengthening the representation of private employers' interests: engineering now has a strong central federation, Federmeccanica, which operates from Rome (like Confindustria) and Milan.

As many industries have companies in both the private and the public sectors, and since both sectors are large in terms of numbers employed, the danger of leapfroging is considerable, and to it may be ascribed the rapid progress into chaos of the collective bargaining structure over the last decade or so.

Structure of trade unions and employers' associations

In both cases, the Confederations are made up of the national associations for each branch of industry — i.e. vertical organisation — and the general regional associations covering all industries. The former deal with the negotiation of terms and conditions for their own industries, while the latter deal with specific regional matters.

Collective bargaining

Apart from recognising the autonomy of the trade unions and employers' associations to make collective agreements regulating the terms and conditions of employment of their members — a provision of the Italian Constitution — the law does not determine the collective bargaining framework. The Constitution does contain certain provisions relating to collective bargaining, but their implementation will be subject to specific laws which have not yet been enacted. In general, legislation has preferred to follow what has been voluntarily agreed, and in some cases to go against the Constitution; for example, the Constitution provides for legislation making collective agreements binding on all firms and employees in a sector subject to the union and the employers' association being recognised as generally representative, but in fact the law of 1959 on this subject continues the situation whereby only members of the bargaining partners are bound by agreements. In the event, such legislation, and the gaps in general labour law, have no effect on the present *de facto* situation.

Collective agreements are concluded at four levels. Separate negotiations take place for private industry and for the semi-public sector (i.e. firms with large or majority holdings by ENI or IRI): in general, the semi-public sector negotiates first, and agreements for both sectors tend to be similar, at 'confederal' and national level.

(1) 'Confederal' level. Agreements between the confederations cover matters affecting employers and employees in all industries throughout the country. At this level, agreements have been made regulating:

— the composition and functions of Works Councils (Commissione Interne)
— individual dismissals and redundancies
— the 'contingency allowance', which accounts for 7-8% of every employee's total remuneration, and which increases in accordance with movements in the cost-of-living index.

(2) National level (by branch of industry). Minimum wage rates and standard conditions of employment are negotiated nationally for two or three years. The original function of the Works Council was to monitor the implementation of agreements at levels 1) and 2), but without further negotiation. For many years, the country was divided into 7 'wage-zones', with a 20% differential between basic rates in zone 0 (industrial north) and zone 6. By agreement this differential has been eliminated; and from the end of 1972 there is a national standard minimum rate for each branch of industry.

Until the beginning of the 1960s, negotiations took place only at these two levels. The formal structure however completely failed to take account of informal (and disorganised) domestic bargaining, which was fairly widespread. Neither the law nor collective agreements at confederal or national level provided for any points to be negotiated at plant level, and consequently no committees or representatives were equipped with the right to negotiate. Similarly, the trade unions had no specific right of access to the establishment. Thus, against a background of traditional paternalism, there was a wide variety of *de facto* negotiating arrangements. Both the trade unions and the employers had an interest in putting order into this situation. A second consideration was the introduction of productivity-based payment systems, which were felt to be necessary in a time of economic expansion. The semi-public engineering agreements therefore, followed by those in the private sector for the same industry and then by other branches, recognised that plant agreements — which however could be concluded only by the appropriate regional or provincial organisations on behalf of their members in the plant — could supplement the national agreements on certain points, including piecerates, new job evaluation systems and productivity bonuses. Although the recession of 1963-65 diminished the importance of introducing new payment methods, the principle behind this 'articulated negotiation' was established that in addition to confederal and national agreements, relatively formal arrangements had been made for negotiation at two other levels.

(3) Local agreements. Agreements at local (regional or provincial) level are thus intended to supplement national provisions. Initially they were intended to keep negotiations out of the factory, in that they could be concluded by the local union and employers' organisations on behalf of their members in individual plants. This became farcical when plant union representatives were delegated with full authority to conclude agreements at local level. In fact, where wage negotiations (ostensibly on productivity-related wages) are concerned, local agreements tended to confuse the situation further when certain branches of industry — particularly the petrochemical sector — made agreements admitting plant negotiations.

(4) Domestic agreements. A number of agreements now recognise plant negotiations in most branches of industry. In the beginning — from 1963 onwards — the subjects of such negotiations were limited to, for example, collective productivity bonuses and the band, as a percentage of earnings, within which these could be fixed. A certain control could thus still be exercised at national level over the burgeoning plant bargaining trend.

Since 1967, however, this control has been negligible. Claims at plant level have gone far outside the limits laid down elsewhere: and matters already decided at national level have widely become the subject of domestic claims. At the same time, the agreed duration of agreements is being ignored, and claims on the same matter are coming up two weeks after the previous settlement. Effectively, therefore, it can be said that agreements made at any level have increasingly become binding on the employer only.

Negotiations at domestic level. There is no established principle which defines *who* shall negotiate on behalf of employees — this differs from factory to factory. It may be the Commissione Interna (Works Council); it may be a body set up under a national agreement, such as the Joint Technical Committees in the engineering industry — which strictly have no negotiating rights; it may be union representatives who, since collective agreements in the late 60s and a law of 1970 (the 'Statuto dei diritti dei Lavoratori') now have the right of access to and representation in plants. Finally, it may be workers' *delegates* — unionised or not — for whom there is no statutory provision, but who occupy an important place in current Italian industrial relations, mainly in the form of 'factory committees'.

The subjects for negotiation have widened, particularly where 'factory committees' (which do not have to bear any responsibility for national agreements) are influential. They cover remuneration, and general terms and conditions; in addition, they may involve claims for job enrichment, abolition of production lines etc. Fiat in particular has recently agreed to discuss such questions.

As a result of increased shopfloor involvement, the trade unions have become more militant and, in recent years have successfully pushed through some fairly detailed and expensive claims, at national level.

Employee representation

Subject to the qualifications mentioned in the preceding section, employees are represented in the following ways.

Commissione Interna (Works Council)

All establishments with more than 40 employees are required to set up a Commissione Interna. (In plants with 5-40 employees, a 'plant delegate' is elected with the same rights and functions as the Commissione Interna). It consists exclusively of employees' representatives, elected on lists of nominations put forward either by trade unions or otherwise.

The Commissione Interna has the function of monitoring the

implementation of national agreements and legal requirements. It must be consulted on the holiday schedule and on the distribution of working hours over the week. It also participates in the establishment of plant welfare arrangements. Its members are not entitled to time off with pay to exercise their functions, but in practice — especially in large firms — they are released for an average of 2 or 3 hours per day. They are also immune from dismissal (except for 'just cause') without the consent of the unions.

Trade union representatives

Since 1970, trade unions have had a legal right to representation in the plant. In firms with 40-200 employees, there is one representative for each trade union with members in the plant; in firms with 201-3000 employees, 1 representative for each union for every 300 employees. In larger firms, the entitlement is one representative for each union for every 500 employees in excess of 3000.

On union business, the trade unions have the right to hold meetings in the plant outside working hours; and, if the three major confederations request it, meetings can be held, with pay, in working hours up to a limit of 10 hours per year for each employee. The unions also receive the right to distribute union information in the factory. Their function within the company, apart from acting on their unions' behalf, is limited: in plants working a five-day week, they have to be consulted on the amount of Saturday overtime working. They can also give support to individual employees, when called upon, in disciplinary matters. Trade union representatives have a right to paid release for 8 hours per month, and unpaid release for 8 hours per year, for trade union business.

Conditions of employment

Remuneration

Payment systems in Italy, in the main, rely on timework and classical piecework. As noted elsewhere, the attempts made in the early 60s to introduce job evaluation and more sophisticated payment structures stagnated in the recession and were then submerged by the period of militancy from 1966 on. The basic hourly minimum rate is the subject of national agreements: it is fixed for manual and staff employees, and for foremen and supervisors. The hourly minimum base-rate, however, is supplemented by a number of allowances and bonuses. These increase the average hourly wage by about a third to a half. Elements of the hourly wage (cf. also the Table on p.55) include:

- basic minimum
- 'contingency allowance'
- seniority bonuses
- other fixed bonuses (e.g. lieu bonus)
- condition allowances
- 'production bonus' (by now, an ordinary bonus, unrelated to output or productivity: agreed domestically)
- Christmas bonus (payment equivalent to a 13th month's pay, paid monthly)
- allowances for hours not worked as a result of the reduction of working hours to 40 per week
- overtime earnings etc.
- piecework earnings (averaging some 4% - 9% above the minimum rate)

Wages

E.E.C. statistics show that increases in both wages and real wages modified by the rise in the cost-of-living index have been higher in Italy than elsewhere in the Six. Between 1964 and 1971 real wages rose by 53%; and annual increases in real wages have been of the order of 20% over the past two or three years. Now that regional differentials have been eliminated in minimum rates, average earnings throughout Italy — including Sicily and Sardinia — are within a narrower band (see Appendix (iii), p.111). There are, however, wide differentials between different branches of industry. (see Appendix (ii), p.110).

Hours of work

The legal maximum for working hours is 48 per week, 8 per day. However, collective agreements in 1969 provided for a reduction of the then standard 44 hours to 40 by the end of 1972. The 5½ day week is standard.

Overtime

For political and collective bargaining reasons, most of Italian industry has adhere᷸ to a basic working week for the past year or two. Overtime is paid at a supplement of 20% for the first two hours and 30% for subsequent hours. This is calculated on the basic rate *plus* usual bonuses and supplements.

Shiftwork and nightwork supplements

Shiftworkers' overtime is paid at 40% for the first and second hours, and 45% thereafter, above the basic rate plus usual supplements. Nightshift workers, and regular nightworkers are paid a supplement of 15%.

Annual and public holidays

Young workers under 16 have an annual holiday entitlement of 30 days; over 16, 20 days.

Collective agreements fix holiday in industry:
  — manual workers: 12-20 days according to seniority (usually the maximum after 20 years service)
  — staff: 12-30 days (maximum at 25 or 20 years' service)
  — management staff: 20-30 days (maximum normally after 10 years service).

Holidays are paid at average earnings: no additional holiday pay is given.

There are 17 paid public holidays in Italy:
New Year's Day	Immaculate Conception
Epiphany	Christmas Day
Easter Monday	Boxing Day
May Day	National holiday (25th April)
Ascension Day	19th March
Corpus Christi	2nd June
Assumption Day	29th June
All Saints	4th November
Local patron saint's day	

Public holidays are paid at average earnings — even when they fall on a normally non-worked day.

Social security

The cost of social security is very high and adds at least 50% to employers' direct wage costs. Insurance is obligatory, and comprehensive. It takes three forms:

(1) a fixed rate, varying according to the level of pay, in the form of a stamp, covering social insurance (total unemployment, disability, old-age etc. — basic schemes). A selective example:

weekly-paid	*value of stamp (lire)*
up to 4000 lire	9
21000-24600	31
35500-39700	50
over 230800	275

monthly paid	
up to 17200	42
90000-106400	136
over 1000000	1185

(2) contributions as a percentage of global earnings including usual bonuses

(3) contributions levied as a percentage of earnings above a minimum of Lit. 500 and a ceiling of Lit. 4000 per day.

These contributions sometimes vary for manual and non-manual employees.

Minimum Social Security Contributions, 1972

Insurance Fund	Type of insurance	manual %	staff %	employer %
INPS	social insurance	—	—	(stamps)
INPS	pensions	6.90	6.90	13.90
INPS	unemployment, TB orphans (ENAOLI)	—	—	4.75
INAM	sickness (manual)	0.15	—	11.93
INAM	sickness (staff)	—	0.15	9.93
INAM	workers' housing (GESCAL)	0.35	0.35	0.70
INAIL	industrial accident	—	—	4-5 (varies)
			of total remuneration incl. bonuses	
INPS	family allowances	—	—	17.50
INPS	earnings compensation fund	—	—	0.20
			of earnings between Lit. 500 and Lit. 4000 daily	

Source: Confindustria, and Labour Ministry.

Total labour costs for the employer are higher than in most countries. The following hypothetical Table, published by Confindustria, gives a useful overview.

Total labour cost of a skilled manual worker in engineering — provinces of
Milan and Turin, May, 1971.   Source: Confindustria

		Lire per hour	As a % of the basic
A —	*Direct pay*		
1.	Contractual minimum	403.20	100.00
2.	piecework supplement	44.35	11.00
3.	production bonus	20.16	5.00
4.	periodic seniority bonuses	12.10	3.00
5.	contingency allowances	44.31	10.99
6.	meal subsidy	1.25	0.31
	A — TOTAL DIRECT PAY	525.37	130.30
B —	*Indirect pay*		
7.	holidays (112 hours x A:1960 [1])	30.02	7.44
8.	paid public holidays (136 hours x A:1960)	36.45	9.04
9.	Christmas bonus (208 hours x A:1960)	55.75	13.83
10.	seniority bonus (88 hours x (A+8%) :1960)	25.47	6.32
11.	reduction in working hours (286 hours x A:1960)	76.66	19.01
12.	paid time off for works meetings (10 hours x A:1960)	2.68	0.66
	B — TOTAL INDIRECT PAY	227.03	56.30
C —	*Insurance and social security contributions*		
13.	social insurance — stamps at 37 lire x 56 [2] : 1960	1.06	0.26
14.	supplementary pensions — 13.90% of A x (2712 [3]) : 1960)	93.78	23.26
15.	unemployment, TB and ENAOLI — 4.75% of A x (2712 : 1960)	34.52	8.56
16.	sickness — 12.46% of A x (2712 : 1960)	90.58	22.46
17.	Workers' housing (GESCAL) — 0.70% of A x (2712 : 1960)	5.09	1.26
18.	industrial accidents — 5% of A x (2712 :1960)	36.35	9.01
19.	associations contribution (0.95% of A x (2712 : 1960)	6.90	1.71
20.	family allowances (15% of 2504 (ceiling) : 1960)	95.82	23.76
21.	earnings compensation fund — 0.20% of 2504 : 1960	1.28	0.32
	C — TOTAL INSURANCE AND SS CONTRIBUTIONS	365.38	90.62
	TOTAL HOURLY COSTS	1117.78	277.23

1)   annual hours actually worked
2)   52 pay-weeks + 4 for Christmas bonus
3)   hours worked plus holidays, Christmas bonus, reduction in working hours and paid time for works meetings = 2712 hours

Total Labour Cost — E.E.C. breakdown for 1969

Manual workers	%
1. Direct wages and regular bonuses	52.66
2. Other bonuses and *ex gratia* payments	7.05
3. Payment for days not worked (holidays etc)	8.25
4. Employers' social security contributions	
— sickness, disability, maternity, retirement, unemployment	19.60
— industrial accidents and diseases	2.34
— family allowances	6.12
— other statutory contributions	0.30
TOTAL, statutory contributions	28.37
— company or sector insurance schemes	0.29
— supplementary retirement pensions	0.16
— contractual or voluntary wage and salary guarantee	—
— supplementary unemployment insurance	—
— contractual supplementary family allowances	0.03
— other contractual or voluntary payments	0.09
TOTAL, contractual and voluntary payments	0.57
TOTAL, employer contributions to social security	28.94
5. Payments in kind	0.18
6. Other payments of a social nature	1.25
7. Training costs	1.20
8. Social taxes	0.47
TOTAL LABOUR COST	100.00

Total Labour Cost — E.E.C. breakdown for 1969

Staff workers	%
1. Direct wages and regular bonuses	55.87
2. Other bonuses and *ex gratia* payments	7.76
3. Payment for days not worked (holidays etc)	10.60
4. Employers' social security contributions	
— sickness, disability, maternity, retirement, unemployment	18.73
— industrial accidents and diseases	0.68
— family allowances	3.66
— other statutory contributions	0.39
TOTAL, statutory contributions	23.46
— company or sector insurance schemes	0.27
— supplementary retirement pensions	0.14
— contractual or voluntary wage and salary guarantee	—
— supplementary unemployment insurance	—
— contractual supplementary family allowances	0.02
— other contractual or voluntary payments	0.14
TOTAL, contractual and voluntary payments	0.56
TOTAL, employer contributions to social security	24.03
5. Payments in kind	0.18
6. Other payments of a social nature	0.86
7. Training costs	0.22
8. Social taxes	0.49
TOTAL LABOUR COST	100.00

3. France

Employment

Recruitment

In France, recruitment involves a certain amount of contact with State authorities; and, while the relevant regulations are not applied with any severe stringency under normal conditions, they must be complied with. Nominally, recruitment is through the national employment service; in some cases, this service is supplemented by other free services, notably those organised by joint bodies representing both sides of industry.

For the liberal professions, public offices, trade associations etc., new engagements are reported by a declaration sent by registered mail within 48 hours to the local office of the Manpower Service (Service de la Main-d'oeuvre).

For industry and commerce, engagements need to be authorized in advance by the Manpower Service. If the Service has not replied within 7 days — 3 in the case of unemployed applicants — it is held to have approved the proposed engagement. This advance authorization is not needed for agricultural workers or those in the entertainment industry. It is also inapplicable when the contract of employment contains a probationary period.

The war-wounded — and persons disabled from whatever cause — have prior claim to 10% of the jobs in a firm. There is also priority — to a percentage laid down by the 'préfet' — for father of three or more children, or widows with at least 2 children to support. Levels of employment of such priority employees must be notified, at least annually, to the Manpower Service, which has the power to impose fines for infringement of the requirement, and also to nominate candidates to fill quotas.

Ex-employees returning from military service (which breaks the contract of employment) have priority in hiring, if, up to a month after completion of their military service, they have notified their former employer (by registered letter) that they wish to be re-employed, and if their job has not disappeared. (Even if it has, they still have priority for a year.)

The employment of foreigners is fairly tightly controlled. To obtain a residence permit (carte de séjour), the worker needs a work permit specifying where, for how long, and in what capacity he is to be employed: the prospective employer must submit two copies of a contract — for a period between three months and a year — to the Manpower Service. Freedom of movement both occupationally and geographically is thereby restricted. Furthermore, quotas operate for foreign workers, varying by occupation and region between 25% and 60%. The quotas may also apply to E.E.C. nationals and citizens of certain French-speaking African states, although in these cases work and residence permits are easier to obtain. In all cases the employer is obliged to register the employment of a foreigner with the Manpower Service.

Works rules. In all establishments in industry and commerce, and in any kind of establishment employing more than 20, Works Rules must be prepared by the employer and forwarded to the Labour Inspector together with the Works Council's opinion. While certain provisions are voluntary, the following are obligatory:

- engagements (documents required etc)
- qualifying tests (for new recruits)
- wage payment, place, method
- schedule of working hours (starting, finishing, clocking etc)
- general conditions at the workplace (lavatories, lockers etc)
- responsibilities in cases of loss or damage to tools or equipment
- safety and hygiene regulations
- periods of notice
- criteria for selecting redundant workers
- disciplinary requirements and measures

The Labour Inspector will amend the Rules in accordance with legal requirements, which must then be registered with the Conseil de Prud'hommes.

Contract of employment

The form. The contract of employment does not need to be in written form, but collective agreements frequently require a statement of the main terms of employment to be given in writing. The contract may not come into effect immediately, if a probationary period has been agreed. The length of such a period is fixed by collective agreement, and varies according to region and job: it is usually a week for manual workers, and one to three months for staffworkers and supervision; three months for management. During the probationary period the contract can be terminated by either party without notice.

Duration. Contracts can be made either for a fixed period or for indeterminate duration. The first case is fairly frequent in agriculture but very rare in industry — for an industrial manual worker, the maximum length of a fixed term contract is one year.

Content. The existence of a contract of employment implies several rights and obligations. The employer is obliged to provide the agreed work, to pay the agreed wages, to observe labour regulations and to ensure that good employer/employee relations exist. He is responsible for the technical and financial running of the enterprise and has statutory managerial rights over the organisation of work. The employee's rights are rather more limited. He is entitled to hold the employer to the performance of his obligations, and also has certain rights pertaining to union activities and representation.

Termination of contract — dismissal and redundancy. Either party may terminate a contract without fixed duration at any time, subject to notice. Termination by either side however requires the prior authorization of the Manpower Service, who must reply within 7 days, or 3 days if termination results from a serious fault justifying summary dismissal. (Tribunals have, however, held that such authorization is unnecessary in the latter case.)

Summary dismissal   An employee may be summarily dismissed without notice for a 'serious fault' (faute grave — tribunals have held this to be constituted by, for example, grossly insulting the foreman etc).

Other dismissals. Once authorization from the   Manpower Service has been received — if the Service fails to reply within 7 days, authorization is held to have been given — the employer must give notice to the employee by registered letter, including the grounds for dismissal. Union membership or political affiliations do not count as ground for dismissals, unless activities connected with them constitute 'serious fault'.

Notice

i) If an employee gives notice, he must respect the periods of notice laid down by collective agreement. In general, these are:

>   *manual* — 1 week
>   *mensualised* (manual on staff conditions) — 2 weeks
>   *staff* — 1 to 3 months according to status.

ii) If an employer gives notice, the periods are:

>   for employees with *less than 6 months' service:* as in i)
>   *6 months' to 2 years' service:* one month (or more if the collective agreement is more generous)
>   *more than 2 years' service:* 2 months, *or* one month and a payment of 10 hours' earnings per year of service with the firm.

Notice may be replaced by payment in lieu, equivalent to what would have been earned in the period, made by whichever party fails to observe the requirement to give notice.

Dismissal allowance. Except in cases of summary dismissal, employees with 2 years' service are entitled to a dismissal allowance of 10 hours' earnings per year of service (or $1/20$ of the monthly wage per year of service in the case of monthly-paid employees). This is the legal minimum. Collective agreements, varying according to region and branch of industry, lay down other provisions which are usually linked to a minimum period of service.

Redundancy. All dismissals, whether individual or collective, count as redundancies where they are caused by economic or technical reasons: and these reasons must be stated when authorisation from the Manpower Service is sought. According to the seriousness of the redundancy, the Works Council must be informed 8 days to three months before application is made, and its opinion taken, although this is not binding on the employer. The employer must take into account any provisions of a collective agreement which applies, and the criteria for selection of redundant workers laid down in the Works Rules. There is no particular redundancy payment. (In development areas, the State may provide transitional allowances to workers undergoing retraining.)

Special protection for Works Council members, Personnel Delegates and union representatives. Members of the Works Council, and

Personnel Delegates, may not be dismissed without the consent of the Works Council. When this consent is not forthcoming, reference must be made to the Labour Inspector.

Union representatives may not be dismissed without the consent of the Labour Inspector.

Limitations. The contract of employment is only suspended in cases of:

- *sickness* (except if it is chronic or where the firm cannot operate properly — in this case notice may be given, or payment in lieu)
- *maternity* (women are not allowed to work in the six weeks following childbirth, or, normally, the two weeks preceding it).

Unlike other European countries, French law holds the contract to be terminated by call-up for military service, although (see *Recruitment)* those returning have priority of re-engagement. Further obligatory military service, however, merely suspends the contract.

Strikes. Participation in a lawful strike does not affect the contract. In general, it should be noted that even when certain regulations are transgressed (such as failure to seek authorization from the Manpower Service), termination of a contract is valid. There is no case where such transgression carries with it the obligation or right of reinstatement.

Work certificate. When an employee leaves, for whatever reason, he has a right to a certificate noting the dates of his employment and the nature of the various jobs he may have held.

Individual disputes. Individual disputes — arising from the contract of employment, dismissals etc — are dealt with through the *conseils de prud'hommes,* which are formed in any town where the need exists. The experts (prud'hommes) who form them are elected for 6 years (renewable for a further 3 years), and come from both sides of industry.

The conseils are in two sections:
(1) a *bureau de conciliation* (conciliation section) consisting of one employer expert and one employee expert.
(2) a *bureau de jugement* (arbitration section) consisting of an equal number of employer and employee experts (the latter divided into manual and staff: at least 2 for each

category). Decisions are reached on a straight majority. In cases of non-decisions, the case is re-examined but this time under the chairmanship of a magistrate. If the subject of dispute is of a value below 2500 F, the decision of the arbitration section is final: if above 2500 F, appeal can be made to a higher court.

Industrial relations

French industrial relations have undergone notable change in the last few years. As in other countries where a large number of small firms support a general employer approach of paternalism, trade unionism has tended towards a general political approach: and the explosions have taken place not so much in connection with collective bargaining (the unions are, in any case, among the weakest numerically in Europe) as in the context of wider protests against the social and political structure. 1968 ultimately brought about a change of Government; and the new Government leaned heavily on the traditional bargaining partners to institute change. Probably the most significant result was the process of 'mensualisation' – the progressive alignment of the status of manual and non-manual employees. This major undertaking is being carried out over several years. In the last few years also, unions have at last obtained access to the plant: and a new minimum wage system links the minimum to increases in the cost of living. But, basically, there have been no radical changes in the structure of collective representation or collective bargaining. The effect of 1968 was certainly to jolt people into action: but once action was commenced, it has proceeded largely according to the old pattern, and without any major concession from employers. The old procedures still appear to operate adequately. Centres of militancy have developed, notably in the Paris region; 1972 had a number of crises. But several trends – the effects of the post-1968 agreements, decentralisation, a strong economic expansion, and the formation of a dynamic 'superministry' for social affairs under M. Edgar Fauré – indicate a settled industrial relations outlook in France for the near future.

Authorities and collective representation

The State. Each *département* has, in addition to the Manpower Service (whose functions have been described in *Recruitment*), its own section of the Labour Inspectorate: these come under the control of some 21 regional directorates. The function of the Labour Inspectors is to ensure the implementation of legislation and regulations covering hygiene and safety, working hours, holidays, employment of women and of children, and workplace representation. They also monitor the application of collective agreements which have been extended to all firms in a sector. Inspectors have the right of access to all establishments; they also work with the medical inspectors and the social security technical committees who are concerned with the laws on hygiene and health matters.

Individual disputes are dealt with by the *conseils de prud'hommes:* collective disputes must, by law, go to conciliation. On national issues, a National Conciliation Committee is formed, on which the Labour Minister and another Minister (for economic affairs) are joined by 4 representatives each of employers and employees; in other cases, regional committees are set up, chaired by the regional director. Mediation can be requested: and if the subject at issue has a bearing on the interpretation of law or an agreement, it can be referred either to litigation or arbitration. The State's role, therefore, is limited: there is no compulsory arbitration, and in the main the State provides for disputes to be sorted out between the parties.

Trade Unions

Membership of trade unions in France probably amounts to only a fifth of the working population. Employees are free to join or not to join: if they do, they will join a member union of one of the major confederations, each of which represents a political tendency. They are:

- *Confédération générale du Travail* (General Confederation of Labour). It has a strong link with the Italian CGIL (with whom it has a co-ordinating committee in Brussels). The CGT bore a somewhat Stalinist complexion for many years, which loyally survived Hungary but was a little shaken by Czechoslovakia — and the 'events' of 1968 in France.
- *Confédération française démocratique du Travail* (French democratic Confederation of Labour). CFDT organises about 25% of union members. It was formed in 1964 on a social-democrat programme as a majority break-away from the CFTC.
- *Confédération Générale du Travail — Force Ouvrière* CGT-FO split off from the CGT to avoid the latter's politics: it has a more moderate Socialist orientation, and organises some 10%

of all union members.

Confédération française des Travailleurs chrétiens (French Confederation of Christian workers). The CFTC is the rump of the CFTC from which the CFDT split in 1964. Its politics are right-of-centre. It has about 5% of the organised labour force.

All these confederations cover both manual and non-manual workers: the *Confédération Générale des Cadres,* which accounts for another 10% of union members, is limited to technical and higher managers.

All these unions count, at national level, as representative bodies. The other unions, which together make up the remaining 10% of organised employees, do not have this status at national level, but may do in individual plants for the purposes of representation at that level. The status of 'most representative' — automatically accorded to the five confederations listed above, and to their affiliates — is necessary in order to sign agreements, particularly where they may be extended.

Employers' associations

The central employers' body is the *Conseil National du Patronat Français* (French National Employers' Council). The CNFP plays a sizeable role in French social and economic life.

Both the employers' and the union confederations consist of members representing a single industry: these in their turn are federations of organisations covering an industry regionally — in many cases, according to *département* — which are usually technically autonomous. At the level of region or *département* they also combine in inter-industry associations.

Collective bargaining

France has two main types of collective agreement: the *ordinary agreement,* which can be signed by any union or unions and any employer, employers or employers' association; and the *extendable agreement,* which needs to be signed by parties with the status of 'most representative' bodies, and can be extended to cover the whole of an industry or region. This latter type of agreement has to follow a detailed format, including treatment of:

— the right to belong to a union and the freedom of opinion
— the wage structure applying to each occupational category

- allowances for dirty and/or dangerous work
- implementation of equal pay for equal work for women and young workers
- conditions of engagement and dismissal
- periods of notice and dismissal allowances
- personnel delegates and Works Council arrangements
- paid leave
- arrangements for termination or revision of the agreement
- agreed conciliation procedures for collective disputes arising from the agreement
- arrangements for apprentices and vocational training
- special conditions of employment for women and young workers

Ordinary agreements are not subject to such regulation of their contents, and may be confined to a single subject. Nevertheless all agreements must be in writing, may be made for a fixed term or indefinite duration, must state the territory and industry covered and must be registered with the *conseil de prud'hommes* of the locality in which they are concluded.

Agreements are extended at the request of a 'most representative' body of either side: they are submitted to the Government committee on collective agreements (Commission supérieure des conventions collectives) consisting of three Ministers, 16 employer and 16 employee representatives and 3 representatives of family interests, which may then extend their provisions to an area, a town, or the whole of an industry, such that all employers, whether members of an association which negotiated the agreement or not, in the designated sector are bound by it. In the case of ordinary agreements, only members of an employers' association are so bound — and must apply the agreement to all their employees.

Agreements are made at several levels. On certain matters they are concluded between the confederations ('accords interprofessionels'), either substantively or as model agreements which will largely be adhered to in national agreements for individual branches of industry. This has been the case, for example, with the process of 'mensualisation' (staff status), where the main guidelines were agreed at 'interprofessionel' level, and the detail was worked out individually for textiles, engineering etc.

At national level — by branch of industry — these matters can also be agreed, as is the case with working hours in the engineering industry. Wages are negotiated at this level in the chemical and textiles industries.

At regional or local level. The engineering industry operates wage agreements at this level.

Agreements can also be made at plant level: in principle, however, plant agreements have the function of adapting agreements made at higher levels to the particular situation in the plant. In this case, the employer must negotiate with the 'most representative' unions in the plant.

As elsewhere, agreements in France set minimum wage rates and conditions, and employers are free to exceed these. A fairly large number of conditions are regulated by law, and provisions less favourable than the legally required minimum cannot be agreed. This applies also to the minimum wage (SMIC).

The collective bargaining structure in France continues to work well. Collectively agreed norms are of basic importance: a high percentage of employers belong to CNPF through its constituent associations, and company agreements are the exception rather than the rule. There are, however, notable exceptions and in this respect the case of Renault is instructive. In the middle 50s, Renault led a move towards company agreements, and was joined by several other companies in this. Most of them have now returned to the more traditional situation, while the original exponent becomes more and more entrammelled in the scenes of ugly militancy which accompany its negotiations.

It is true that there was some increase in plant bargaining (as opposed to company bargaining) during the events of 1968 and afterwards (following the Grenelle agreements). But this has yet to show up as a major trend in French bargaining patterns generally.

Conditions of employment

Remuneration

Payment systems in France are mainly timework, classical piecework and premium (fixed basic with output-related bonus). Job evaluation schemes are a growing feature in a number of firms, but there are no agreed formulae for JE systems at national or local level. As in the UK, pay systems are geared to produce an average weekly rate. Under the mensualisation agreements, there is a growing tendency to pay wages by the month, although in principle wages must be paid at least every 16 days. The same agreement may well ultimately have the effect of producing uniform pay schemes for all personnel, which may bring about more rapid growth in job evaluation. Under the agreements, certain bonuses —

e.g. seniority bonuses of up to 10% of basic wage for 10 years of service paid to staff in some sectors — will be progressively applied to 'mensualised' manual workers.

The index-linked minimum guaranteed wage (SMIC). The rate of the SMIC is fixed by the Government after consulting the Collective Agreements Committee. It can change in three circumstances:

(i) Any variation of more than 2% in the cost-of-living index is matched by an equivalent increase in the SMIC.

(ii) At the beginning of July every year, changes in the purchasing power of the franc (measured on a 'shopping basket' principle) are compared with wage movements over the equivalent period, and, in certain cases, the SMIC can be increased.

(iii) The Government may increase the SMIC even when the cost-of-living has not increased; or it may increase it by more than the increase in the cost-of-living.

There is a further possibility: the Government may freeze the SMIC, as in September 1972. The SMIC represents an absolute minimum: its level has tended to be 65%-70% of average hourly earnings in industry.

Minimum contractual wage. A minimum rate is agreed in wage negotiations at national or regional level for the various categories of workers — thus in engineering there are two unskilled categories, two semi-skilled and three skilled. These categories may vary by region, even in that industry. The agreement will usually give some indication of the relationship of the minima to domestic rates (fixed by the employer), such that for pieceworkers, for example, a kind of minimum earnings level, above the minimum agreed rate, is provided for.

Wages

The increase in real wages in France between 1964 and 1971 was 37% according to E.E.C. statistics: the net annual rate in the past two or three years however has been around 7%, and inflation is becoming a major problem (with wages increasing at about 12-13%, but prices close behind).

Earnings are predictably higher in the Paris region than elsewhere: the south, the east, and the outer Paris area form an intermediate earnings band: and the north lags behind (see Appendix (iii) p.111).

Women's earnings represent around three-quarters of men's. (For sector differentials, see Appendix (ii), p.110.)

Working hours

The 40-hour week has been in effect since a law of 1936. Up to 20 hours of overtime per week are allowed. Calculated over a 12-week period, however, 54 hours are the maximum for a week. The CNPF and the unions have agreed a framework whereby working hours are being gradually reduced (e.g. initially by 1-2 hours where average hours exceeded 45), and sector agreements have put this into effect. In terms of regular overtime, the majority of workers (almost half) have a working week of around 46 hours; two-fifths work 41-45 hours (manufacturing sector). The building industry tends to work considerably more overtime than most sectors.

In most industries, overtime is paid at time and a quarter for hours between 40 and 48, and time and half thereafter — the weekly hours being the basis of calculation.

Shiftwork and nightwork supplements

Provisions for shiftwork and nightwork vary by region and branch of industry. There is no supplement for dayshift working: nightshift usually carries a supplement of 15%-20%, and regular nightwork a supplement of 15%-50%.

Annual holidays

Legislation guarantees 2 working days per month every year: the normal entitlement is therefore 4 weeks (of 6 working — or 'workable' — days). At least two weeks are to be taken together, preferably between 1st May and the 31st October. When the entitlement is only up to 12 days (because the credit system operates from June to June), it must be taken as a single block. There is no collectively agreed additional holiday pay.

Public holidays

Only May Day is a statutory holiday with pay. 6-10 of the public holidays are paid by collective agreement. Others require to be recovered or are treated as unpaid leave. The days are:

New Year's Day	Assumption Day
Easter Monday	All Saints Day
May Day	Christmas Day
Ascension Day	14th July (Bastille)
Whit Monday	11th November (Armistice)

Paid public holidays are compensated with full average earnings. The number of paid days varies by sector and region, e.g. Paris in general has 8 days, mensualised workers in engineering have all 10 etc.

Social security

The social security system in France is, as in other European countries, based on the insurance principle. It is extremely comprehensive: and the cost to the employer is some 20-30% of total labour cost. There are two main systems:

(a) the State system, which through several organisations, administers: unemployment insurance; retirement and disability insurance; health insurance; death insurance; family allowances; industrial accidents. The State system is obligatory for all employed persons;

(b) industry-wide supplementary systems, set up by collective agreement, providing supplementary benefits for retirement, unemployment, family allowances etc. Two such large systems — both set up and administered jointly by the CNPF and the unions — are AGIRC (providing supplementary retirement pensions) for management staff, and UNIRS, which provides the same for other employed persons.

Additionally, companies are free to arrange further benefits for their employees.

These systems are too numerous and individually too complicated to be described here. However, although some of the rates have risen slightly, the E.E.C. breakdown of labour costs for 1969 gives an idea of the contributions for individual insurable items.

Total Labour Cost — E.E.C. breakdown for 1969

Manual Workers	%
1. Direct wages and regular bonuses	60.23
2. Other bonuses and *ex gratia* payments	2.44
3. Payment for days not worked (holidays etc.)	8.35
4. Employers' social security contributions	
— sickness, disability, maternity, retirement, unemployment	11.30
— industrial accidents and diseases	3.16
— family allowances	7.31
— other statutory contributions	0.33
TOTAL, statutory contributions	22.11
— company or sector insurance schemes	0.20
— supplementary retirement pensions	2.01
— contractual or voluntary wage and salary guarantee	0.18
— supplementary unemployment insurance	0.23
— contractual supplementary family allowances	0.09
— other contractual or voluntary payments	0.15
TOTAL, contractual and voluntary payments	2.86
TOTAL, employer contributions to social security	24.97
5. Payments in kind	1.63
6. Other payments of a social nature	1.61
7. Training costs	0.76
8. Social taxes	—
TOTAL LABOUR COST	100.00

Total Labour Cost — E.E.C. breakdown for 1969

Staff Employees	%
1. Direct wages and regular bonuses	62.19
2. Other bonuses and *ex gratia* payments	5.02
3. Payment for days not worked (holidays etc.)	8.07
4. Employers' social security contributions	
— sickness, disability, maternity, retirement, unemployment	8.33
— industrial accidents and diseases	1.69
— family allowances	5.13
— other statutory contributions	0.14
TOTAL, statutory contributions	15.30
— company or sector insurance schemes	0.21
— supplementary retirement pensions	4.46
— contractual or voluntary wage and salary guarantee	0.34
— supplementary unemployment insurance	0.24
— contractual supplementary family allowances	0.09
— other contractual or voluntary payments	0.20
TOTAL, contractual and voluntary payments	5.54
TOTAL, employer contributions to social security	20.84
5. Payments in kind	1.49
6. Other payments of a social nature	1.70
7. Training costs	0.69
8. Social taxes	
TOTAL LABOUR COST	100.00

Employee representation

Two members of the labour-force, appointed by the Works Council, attend meetings of the Board (Conseil d'administration) in an advisory capacity: they do not vote. Employee representation in France is otherwise through the Works Council, the Personnel Delegates or the trade union 'sections', all of which enjoy consultative and information rights. If these rights seem limited, one should remember the considerable extent of 'paritarisme' at national level and regional level which appears in the jointly-operated conciliation machinery, and in a variety of schemes instituted by collective agreement, such as the supplementary social security arrangements. Lastly, there is a trend to co-operation in State bodies, of which the Collective Agreements Committee is an example. Recent Governments have encouraged this trend, which is probably why the mensualisation provisions were agreed rather than enacted.

Representation in the plant

Works Council (Comité d'Entreprise). Establishments with more than 50 employees must set up a Works Council consisting of one management representative (the employer) who takes the Chair and a number of employee representatives which varies from 3 to 11 for more than 10,000 employees. The latter are elected for two years on lists of candidates nominated by the trade unions. In the event of a second ballot (e.g. if less than half of the electorate vote in the first), any candidate may stand. Time spent in meetings is paid, and members of the Works Council may be additionally released for up to 20 hours per month. The Council has rights of consultation and information on major policy decisions, such as redundancies; and information rights on general economic and financial matters — they must be provided with the same information as the shareholders. The Council is also consulted on various internal administrative questions (domestic welfare and training programmes).

Personnel Delegates (Délégués du personnel). Firms with more than 10 employees must release personnel delegates up to 15 hours per month. They are elected for one year in the same manner as members of the Works Council; and range from 1 delegate in firms with 11-25 employees to 9 delegates in firms with 500-1000. The delegate's function is to make representations on individual (or collective) claims arising from labour legislation, wage rates, occupational classification etc. They are also obliged to report transgressions of the law to the Labour Inspector, and generally to co-operate with him.

Trade union sections (sections syndicales). In establishments with more than 50 employees, the 'most representative' unions in the plant may set up union 'sections'. These have, however, few functions as such, and have more the nature of diplomatic representation. The law establishing the *sections syndicales* does allow internal union activities to be carried on, but to a limited extent.

Safety and hygiene committee (comité d'hygiène et de sécurité). This joint committee is set up in establishments with more than 50 employees, the employee members being appointed by the Works Council. It meets at least every three months, and monitors the implementation of safety regulations.

These are the legal requirements: the effectiveness and the relative importance of these committees will depend very much on the situation in the individual plant. The committees mainly have the function of monitoring the application of questions regulated or agreed at other levels, but the system is flexible. It nicely apportions potential bargaining rights to the 'most representative' union, even while it continues to try to stress the distinction between union representatives as such and union representatives filling positions on 'constitutional' bodies designed to represent the whole of the personnel rather than sectional interests.

4. Belgium

Employment

Contracts

Belgian law distinguishes between manual and staff employees.

Manual workers. The contract can be concluded verbally, but must be in writing if it is a probationary contract (7-14 days) or for a fixed term.

Notice is:
less than 6 months' service	7 days
6 months'-10 years' service	14 days
10-20 years' service	28 days
over 20 years	56 days

Staff employees. The contract is usually in writing.

Notice:
for employees earning less
than 150,000 FB p.a.   3 months for every 3 years' service
for employees earning more
than 150,000 FB p.a.   varies: minimum of 3 months for every 3 years' service

Serious faults (fautes graves) may be subject to summary dismissal without notice. Notice must be given in writing.

Redundancy. There is a distinction between plant closure and collective dismissal (reduction of the workforce by 20% in a week). In the first case, the Works Council must be informed at once, as must the National Employment Office, the relevant ministries and public services, and the Joint Commission for the industry. Two types of indemnity may be paid to redundant workers: one paid either by the employer or from a redundancy fund to which he contributes, giving 1,000 FB per year of service up to 20,000 FB. An additional payment of 1,000 FB per year-of-age above 45 made. The second type of payment is made by the State, which for a period compensates the loss of earnings, or subsidizes the transition to a lower wage.

Industrial relations

Trade unions

About 70% of the Belgian labour force belong to the three main unions, each of which is designated a 'most representative' body.

- CSC (Confédération des Syndicats Chrétiens/Confederation of Christian Unions) represents about 50% of union members: it has very strong support in Flemish areas.
- FGTB (Fédération Générale du Travail de Belgique/Belgian General Federation of Labour) covers around 45% of all organised employees, and is Socialist in character.
- CGSLB (Centrale Générale des Syndicats Libéraux de Belgique/ Central Organisation of Belgian Liberal Unions)

Employers' associations

The FIB (Fédération des Industries Belges/Federation of Belgian Industry) is the central body, made up of the associations covering each branch of industry, of which there are 41.

Collective bargaining

Wages and conditions are negotiated according to the principle termed 'social programming', which in the main is strictly adhered to. The structure of collective bargaining and the regulation of industrial relations is as follows:

(a) Conseil National du Travail (National Labour Council). The Conseil National consists of 22 members, from both sides of industry, with a Government-appointed Chairman. It has an advisory function, and may act on references from the Government or on its own initiative. The Conseil does not negotiate, nor does it have any

power to lay down regulations; but its recommendations carry weight, and the Government is obliged to consult it on legislative matters bearing on conditions of employment. The Conseil also mediates when national negotiations reach deadlock.

(b) Agreements covering all branches of industry. These can be signed by the FIB and the three unions: but they do *not* cover wages. They may however deal with general working conditions, such as holidays or joint working hours.

(c) Commissions Paritaires (Joint Commissions). These are joint negotiating committees for each branch of industry, and consist of the appropriate employers' association and trade unions. Wage rates are agreed at this level for each sector, and also conditions to meet the special requirements of a particular industry. Most wage agreements include a clause linking the minimum to movements in the cost-of-living increase ($\pm$ 2%). These agreements will also specify how they are to be applied in the plant.

Collective agreements are closely adhered to. In many cases, they are made generally applicable within a branch of industry by Royal decree. Recently, however, the process of negotiating the agreements has proved less smooth: in the engineering sector in 1971 national negotiations broke down and agreements were finally concluded at regional level.

Conditions of employment

Real wages rose by 42% between 1964 and 1971: over the last few years, the annual rate has been around 7-9%. (For differentials between sectors, see Appendix (ii), p.110).

The *standard working week* is now 41 hours, which will be reduced to 40 by 1975. A 5-day week is worked. In 1971, average overtime in manufacturing industry was 2.2 hours per week. Overtime, calculated on daily working time, is paid at time and a quarter for the first two hours and time and a half thereafter. There are no agreed bonuses or allowances for nightwork and shiftwork; the practice varies widely.

The *annual holiday entitlement* is 17 days in 1972, rising to 20 days in 1973. It is paid at average earnings plus a bonus equivalent to 3 weeks pay.

Belgian workers enjoy 10 paid *public holidays:*

New Year's Day	Assumption
Easter Monday	All Saints Day
May Day	Christmas Day
Ascension Day	21st July (Independence Day)
Whit Monday	11th November (Armistice Day)

Social security

The Belgian social security system is comprehensive and covers all employed persons. Contributions are payable to the ONSS (Office National de la Sécurité Sociale) as follows:

Manual workers	ceiling	employer %	employee %	total %
Unemployment		1.70	1.20	2.90
Sickness/disability	16,075	1.80	1.20	3.00
Family allowances	FB per	10.50	—	10.50
Industrial diseases	month	0.75	—	0.75
		14.75	2.40	17.15
Health	26,575 FB per month	2.00	3.75	5.75
Retirement/death	none	8.00	6.00	14.00
Annual holiday bonus		6.00	—	6.00
		14.00	6.00	20.00

(Situation in 1972)

An analogous scheme covers staff employees. The contribution ceilings vary according to movements in the cost-of-living index.

Total Labour Cost — E.E.C. breakdown for 1969

Manual Workers	%
1. Direct wages and regular bonuses	63.43
2. Other bonuses and *ex gratia* payments	2.54
3. Payment for days not worked (holidays etc)	11.01
4. Employers' social security contributions	
— sickness, disability, maternity, retirement, unemployment	10.35
— industrial accidents and diseases	2.93
— family allowances	6.51
— other statutory contributions	0.89
TOTAL, statutory contributions	20.68
— company or sector insurance schemes	0.05
— supplementary retirement pensions	0.20
— contractual or voluntary wage and salary guarantee	0.06
— supplementary unemployment insurance	—
— contractual supplementary family allowances	0.04
— other contractual or voluntary payments	0.08
TOTAL, contractual and voluntary payments	0.43
TOTAL, employer contributions to social security	21.11
5. Payments in kind	0.41
6. Other payments of a social nature	1.22
7. Training costs	0.28
8. Social taxes	—
TOTAL LABOUR COST	100.00

Total Labour Cost — E.E.C. breakdown for 1969

Staff Employees	%
1. Direct wages and regular bonuses	63.30
2. Other bonuses and *ex gratia* payments	7.57
3. Payment for days not worked (holidays etc)	12.04
4. Employers' social security contributions	
— sickness, disability, maternity, retirement, unemployment	6.12
— industrial accidents and diseases	1.25
— family allowances	4.92
— other statutory contributions	0.08
TOTAL, statutory contributions	12.37
— company or sector insurance schemes	3.37
— supplementary retirement pensions	—
— contractual or voluntary wage and salary guarantee	—
— supplementary unemployment insurance	—
— contractual supplementary family allowances	—
— other contractual or voluntary payments	—
TOTAL, contractual and voluntary payments	3.37
TOTAL, employer contributions to social security	15.74
5. Payments in kind	0.48
6. Other payments of a social nature	0.74
7. Training costs	0.12
8. Social taxes	—
TOTAL LABOUR COST	100.00

Employee representation

Works Council (Conseil d'Entreprise)

The Works Council is obligatory in firms employing more than 150. It consists of management representatives and employee representatives up to a ratio of 50:50. The employee representatives are elected on nominations put forward by the most representative unions. The Works Council has rights of information on levels of production and the company's economic situation every quarter, and a full report must be made at the end of the financial year. It must be informed and consulted on matters concerning employment, personnel policies and vocational training; and it administers certain welfare arrangements, and the holiday schedule.

Safety and Hygiene Committee

This is a joint committee which is obligatory in establishments with more than 50 employees.

Union delegation (Délégation Syndicale du Personnel)

Both manual workers and staff workers are, since 1971, entitled to a union delegation which can negotiate on their behalf on issues not settled in collective agreement — particularly wage grades. The delegations vary in size depending on the size of the labour force: 2-21 members for manual workers, 2-6 for staff employees. A number of hours is credited every month, again depending on the size of the firm, for the delegations to exercise their functions.

5. Netherlands

Employment

Recruitment

There are no regulations concerning recruitment: the State does, however, operate an employment service. Similarly, while employers are encouraged to employ disabled or handicapped workers, there is no obligation to do so.

Contract of employment

Form. There is no obligatory form of contract, but it is usual to give a statement of the main terms.

Duration. The contract is usually of indeterminate duration.

Content. In most cases, the terms and conditions of a contract are those of the current collective agreements. In other cases, they are the subject of individual arrangements.

Termination — dismissal — redundancy

Termination of a contract of employment is subject to notice, which may be given verbally. The legal periods of notice may be lengthened or shortened by collective agreement:

age 21 and over:	at least the period between 2 pay dates — 1 week per year of service (maximum 13 weeks)
age 45 and over:	additional week per year of service after age 45 to a maximum of 13 weeks (total: 26)
age 50 and over, with minimum 1 year service:	minimum 3 weeks

Dismissals may be either with notice or, for 'urgent reasons', summary dismissal without notice. Except where the dismissal is mutually acceptable, the employer must seek the authorization of the regional employment office. Even where this has been given, the employee may appeal to the local court to find that he has been unfairly dismissed (for 'manifestly unreasonable' grounds). If he is upheld, the dismissal is invalid and he must be reinstated.

There is no specific provision for *redundancy,* which is loosely defined as 'a relatively high number of dismissals in a short period'. These must, in the usual way, be authorized by the regional employment office: a guideline set down by the employers' organisations recommends prior warning to the office, and discussions with the unions in the plant. Provisions for redundancy pay are not widespread, although there is such an agreement for the printing industry.

Limitations

Employees may not be dismissed during sickness, and the contract is not terminated during military service (if the employee has one year's service) or in certain special circumstances (such as death of a relative etc.).

Industrial relations

For many years following the end of the war, industrial relations in the Netherlands were subject to extremely tight, centralised control exercised by the Government with the close co-operation of employers and trade unions. It is a measure of the degree of consensus achieved that this system, which incorporated an incomes policy under which minimum agreed rates were also maximum rates, operated successfully through rapid economic expansion and full employment until the early 60s.

The system was initiated in the years following the war as part of a general control of the economy. Increases in wages were uniformly controlled by the Government and based on overall industrial productivity. After 1950 (the Organisation of Industry Act), a complex procedure was developed which involved a number of bodies in the determination of wage increases — the Board of Government Mediators (Government-appointed but independent), the Central Planning Office, the Social and Economic Council (a tripartite body — see below), and the Labour Foundation (a joint employer/union body — see below). When general guidelines had been agreed, they were incorporated into the agreements for each branch of industry

This system began to weaken during the 50s, as controls in other areas of the economy were gradually relaxed, until in 1959 productivity by branch of industry was substituted for overall productivity as the criterion of relative wage-rates. These developments, and the connected factor that more and more firms were paying 'black rates' — i.e. above the standard — in view of the shortage of labour, led to widespread and overt disregard of the norms laid down centrally, and a wages explosion took place. The credibility of the central bodies was then further eroded when the effects of the wages explosion were fully compensated by an unexpected 'productivity explosion'. From then on, collective agreements submitted to the central authorities for confirmation appeared merely to be rubber-stamped. This situation persisted until 1969 when the introduction of VAT sent prices soaring. In the same year, the Government, employers and unions agreed a ceiling for wages for 1970; but before the return to central negotiation could be tested, the Government introduced a Wages Act, without consulting the other parties, which empowers it to freeze wages in certain circumstances and also to modify the provisions of individual agreements as it sees fit. These provisions remain in force. In 1970, attempts to return to tripartite consultations came to nothing, and the Government introduced a wages freeze in 1971, in an effort to contain an inflationary spiral which nevertheless continues.

Recent events have shown that there is still a need for central control of wages to be at least possible in the Netherlands. One effect of the laissez-faire years (1963-1969) however was to transfer the emphasis in the collective bargaining structure to the branch-of-industry negotiating level, such that the individual industrial unions gained in significance while the central confederations lost. Additionally, regional and sectional disparities have led to occasional militant action at plant-level. Tensions between the various levels of union organisation have led the confederations — who also for political reasons seek to re-establish central control — to consider a merger, and to set up a more aggressive programme of claims.

Although the situation of full employment and scarcity of skilled labour which caused employers to be largely instrumental in rocking the boat in the 1960s shows no sign of easing, there is every probability that inflation, if not contained, will cause them too to seek a return to central control. It remains a curious fact that, given the situation, plant or company bargaining did not develop significantly after 1963, and that ever fewer collective agreements were concluded in the Netherlands covering ever larger numbers of employees over the period. In fact, employers found a different way of attracting skilled manual labour. Since 1965, firms have been instituting an 'integrated' status for their employees by applying staff conditions generally. Most sectors have now agreed that integration will be introduced in all firms within the next few years; but in the late sixties, many firms preferred the medium-term advantage of integration to the short-term advantages of 'competitive' wage-rates.

If industrial relations in the Netherlands are in a state of flux, they are still orderly by the standards of other countries. The institutions set up to administer the wage policy which was vital to post-war reconstruction still operate (with some exceptions), and the collective bargaining structure in general remains intact, even though the emphasis has currently shifted away from the central bodies. Nevertheless, the recent developments (not least the employers' initiative on integration) have prepared the ground for rationalisation of the structure, and a lot will depend on the unions' strategies, both internal as well as external.

Trade Unions

Dutch trade unions are grouped in three central confederations:

- NVV (Nederlands Verbond van Vakverenigingen/Netherlands Federation of Trade Unions) consists of 16 member unions covering around 575,000, and has a social-democrat complexion. The NVV has been more militant and more ready to take industrial action than the other two confederations.
- NKV (Nederlands Katholiek Vakverbond/Netherlands Catholic Federation of Trade Unions) with 19 member unions representing about 400,000 workers.
- CNV (Christelijk National Vakverbond/Federation of Protestant Christian Trade Unions) has a membership of 238,000 in 22 unions.

(NB membership of a denominational union is not dependent on religious belief, nor are these organisations particularly 'religious' themselves. Their broad ethical outlook, however, is marked by their denominational character.)

Now that their member unions have emerged as powerful negotiators in their own right, the three confederations have formed a co-operative body to establish common policies. Previously, their involvement in the bipartite and tripartite bodies was the focus for their co-operation. Their present policies include a return to centrally controlled wage determination, increased co-determination for their members (involving also an increase in the powers of the Works Council), improved working conditions, higher pensions, special privileges for union members.

Employers' associations

Two main confederations, the VNO (Verbond van Nederlandse Ondernemingen/Federation of Netherlands Industry) and the NCW (Nederlands Christelijk Werkgeversverbond/Netherlands Christian Employers' Federation), represent respectively the non-denominational and the Christian associations for each branch of industry. Both at confederal level, and at branch-of-industry level, there is close co-operation. In some industries there is now a single association representing all leanings: and employers have often found it useful to belong to associations of each tendency.

Labour Foundation (*Stichting van der Arbeid*)

The Labour Foundation is a joint organisation set up privately by the trade unions and the employers' associations. It had considerable importance in its advisory role, which the Government recognised, when strict wage control was exercised, but in recent years this function has lost its significance. Nevertheless, the Foundation continues to provide a forum for joint consultations both on wages policy and on other matters relating to employment, such as for example the question of pensions.

The Social and Economic Council

The Council consists of 15 representatives each from unions and employers' organisations, and 15 Government nominees. In reports made twice a year, the Council sets out recommendations to the bargaining partners on general wage-cost guidelines.

Collective bargaining

Agreements in sectors consisting of a large number of small under-takings (e.g. agriculture) are frequently made through an Industrial Board which can effectively turn an agreement into a statutory regulation. In most of industry, however, this does not happen. Agreements are made by unions and employers or employers' associations for a duration of up to 5 years, although the average is 1-3 years. Following the lead of the engineering agreement, some agreements now include an escalator clause but frequently a limit (e.g. 6% p.a.) is included, so that any increase in the cost-of-living above the limit will not be met automatically, but will incur new negotiations.

Under the Wage Act, wage agreements must be registered with the Ministry of Social Affairs, who may declare certain provisions ineffective if they conflict with the Government's assessment of the economic situation.

On application from one of the parties, the Minister for Social Affairs has the authority to extend the application of a collective agreement to all firms and employees in that sector if he so decides and if a majority of employees are already covered by the agreement.

Collective agreements cover terms and conditions of employment and also such matters as occupational pension schemes, training, disputes procedures at plant and national level etc.

Dutch law does not distinguish between manual and non-manual employees and in practice only the NKV applies the distinction. There remain some differences resulting from contractual arrange-ments, but these should gradually disappear as 'integration' becomes the rule rather than the exception in Dutch industry.

Conditions of employment

Remuneration

Real earnings in the Netherlands rose by 39% between 1964 and 1971, which conceals the highest rises in the Six both in gross wages and in the cost-of-living. There is a noticeable differential between earnings in the industrial triangle bounded by Rotterdam, Amsterdam and Utrecht (the provinces of North and South Holland and Utrecht) and the other provinces of the Netherlands. (See Appendix (iii) p.111.) (For sector differentials, see Appendix (ii), p.110.) The main trend in payment systems is away from PBR.

The period of strict wages control predictably encouraged the development of a variety of techniques of personal assessment etc., and job evaluation was a technique subject to central control of criteria. There are, however, separate systems for manual and non-manual employees: where the integrated status is in operation, a conversion system operates to align categories. Additional remuneration comes in the form of asset formation for employees, which takes different forms in different agreements or companies.

Working hours

Hours of work are currently 42½, for all employees, although in practice office staff tend to work shorter hours. In 1971, average hours worked were 43.8 in manufacturing, 44.1 in construction, with no individual sector working very much more overtime than any other. The 5-day week is usual in industry, and overtime (above 8½ hours per day) is paid at time and a quarter for the first two hours and time and a half thereafter. Three-and four-shift systems are sometimes worked: in these cases, the 2nd, 3rd and 4th shifts are paid at an additional 10-20% (laid down by industry agreement, or regulated in the plant).

Annual holidays

The legal minimum holiday entitlement is two weeks, but in general three weeks are the usual minimum. These are often increased by years of age and/or years of service: the engineering entitlement is 17-22 days.

Holidays are paid at average earnings, and an additional bonus of at least 6% per month. Frequently this bonus is credited at 6.4% of monthly pay, thus giving a 100% additional holiday pay: in some agreements, the credit is even 6.8%.

Public holidays

There are 7 paid public holidays:

New Year's Day	Christmas Day
Easter Monday	Boxing Day
Ascension Day	National holiday (30th April)
Whit Monday	

Social Security

The Netherlands have a comprehensive insurance system, covering retirement, disability, death, family allowances, unemployment, sickness. The general schemes are financed by contributions, the employee paying the entire contribution for retirement pensions and death benefits (which cover all Netherlands citizens and not only employed persons); the employer paying the entire contribution for family allowances; and the other elements being shared. The contributions are payable only up to an earnings ceiling of 18,800 fl. − 25,000 fl. p.a. There are a number of contractual or voluntary arrangements which have been set up and are administered jointly under collective agreement either at company or branch-of-industry level. This is especially the case for supplementary retirement pensions. Like the UK, the Netherlands suffer from a number of inadequate benefits deriving from the general schemes, which are generally not earnings-linked and are certainly not inflation-proof.

Total Labour Cost — E.E.C. breakdown for 1969

Manual Workers	%
1. Direct wages and regular bonuses	61.75
2. Other bonuses and *ex gratia* payments	2.77
3. Payment for days not worked (holidays etc)	10.68
4. Employers' social security contributions	
— sickness, disability, maternity, retirement, unemployment	
— industrial accidents and diseases	} 11.01
— family allowances	3.93
— other statutory contributions	—
TOTAL, statutory contributions	14.94
— company or sector insurance schemes	0.69
— supplementary retirement pensions	3.13
— contractual or voluntary wage and salary guarantee	0.49
— supplementary unemployment insurance	—
— contractual supplementary family allowances	0.09
— other contractual or voluntary payments	0.07
TOTAL, contractual and voluntary payments	4.46
TOTAL, employer contributions to social security	19.40
5. Payments in kind	0.46
6. Other payments of a social nature	3.66
7. Training costs	1.27
8. Social taxes	—
TOTAL LABOUR COST	100.00

Total Labour Cost — E.E.C. breakdown for 1969

Staff Employees	%
1. Direct wages and regular bonuses	60.18
2. Other bonuses and *ex gratia* payments	6.89
3. Payment for days not worked (holidays etc)	10.88
4. Employers' social security contributions	
— sickness, disability, maternity, retirement, unemployment	7.63
— industrial accidents and diseases	
— family allowances	3.36
— other statutory contributions	—
TOTAL, statutory contributions	10.99
— company or sector insurance schemes	0.75
— supplementary retirement pensions	6.48
— contractual or voluntary wage and salary guarantee	0.43
— supplementary unemployment insurance	—
— contractual supplementary family allowances	0.06
— other contractual or voluntary payments	0.06
TOTAL, contractual and voluntary payments	7.79
TOTAL, employer contributions to social security	18.78
5. Payments in kind	0.48
6. Other payments of a social nature	2.34
7. Training costs	0.45
8. Social taxes	—
TOTAL LABOUR COST	100.00

Employee representation

Supervisory Board

Under a law of 1971, companies with a capital of 10 million fl. and 100 employees will be required from July 1973 to institute a Supervisory Board consisting of shareholders', management and employees' representatives. No group has any absolute right to be represented, nor will they be represented as *groups*. Appointment will be by co-option to the existing Board on nominations from the shareholders, the Works Council, the Management Board or the Supervisory Board itself. Both the shareholders and the Works Council may veto the appointment of a member.

Works Council (Ondernemingsrad)

Establishments with more than 100 employees are required to set up a Works Council chaired by the employer. The Works Council has no specified number of members, but it must have at least 3. Members are elected from nominations put forward either by unions or by other groups of employees.

The Works Council checks on the operation of safety and hygiene regulations: it also sets up the holiday schedule and negotiates the distribution of working hours. It must be consulted on all major decisions (mergers, shutdown, reorganization) which affect the personnel (in the case of shutdown, the employer must agree a 'social plan' with the unions), and dismissals in general. It should also be consulted on matters connected with remuneration. The Council must also be informed on the economic situation.

Unions at plant-level

While union members have always had a representative (vertrouwensman) in the plant, until recently he had no active role. The unions are currently trying to re-define the role of the union in the plant, and a lead has been set by the recent engineering agreement, which recommended that plant negotiations might be considered with union representatives. The same agreement widened the union's access to its members at plant-level: this trend seems likely to continue.

6. Luxembourg

Employment

Recruitment

Employers are obliged to give details of unfilled vacancies to the National Labour Office. Normally, recruitment takes place through the Office, and in all cases it has to be informed of engagements. Employers may be required to reserve up to 2% of available jobs for disabled workers.

Contract of employment

Form. For manual workers, the contract does not need to be written unless it contains provision for a probationary period. For staff employees the contract is in writing.

Duration. For both manual and non-manual workers, the contract is usually of indefinite duration.

Termination – dismissal – redundancy

Contracts may be *terminated* by notice: the legal minimum period is 2 weeks where notice is given by a manual worker. Notice given by employer must be at least:

Manual workers:
up to 5 years' service	4 weeks
5-10 years' service	8 weeks
more than 10 years	12 weeks

Staff employees:
up to 5 years' service	2 months
5-10 years' service	4 months
more than 10 years	6 months

(Manual workers may be given notice of 12, 20 and 24 weeks according to service if, in firms employing under 20, the employer opts for this rather than payment of severance pay.)

Dismissals, whether with notice or without (for 'serious faults'), must be notified by registered letter (in the latter case, the employee can ask for the reasons, in writing). The Employee Delegates must be informed in advance, and dismissals must be notified to the National Labour Office. Dismissals will not be judicially upheld if they represent an 'economically or socially abnormal' act.

There are few provisions for *redundancy* situations as such. In the case of collective dismissals (more than 10 employees within 30 days), the Employee Delegates must be informed in advance, as must the National Labour Office. Dismissals may not take effect for six weeks after the Office has been informed, and this period may be extended by the Ministry of Labour. There is no special redundancy payment beyond severance pay.

Severance pay

    Manual workers:
    5 years' service   1 month's pay
    10 years' service   2 months' pay
    15 years' service   3 months' pay
    Staff employees:
    15 years' service   3 months' pay
    20 years' service   6 months' pay
    25 years' service   9 months' pay

Industrial relations

Collective agreements in Luxembourg are agreed freely between the parties, but in some cases (sectors of the economy with a number of small firms) these can be extended by the Minister of Labour to be applicable to the whole sector. The main industries are covered by voluntary agreements; frequently these industries are dominated by one very large company. ARBED, the iron and steel company, is the largest employer not only in its industry but also in Luxembourg as a whole, and its influence on the collective agreements in iron and steel and engineering is overwhelming.

Collective agreements are concluded at industry or company level with the relevant section of the Fédération Nationale des Ouvriers de Luxembourg. They regulate wages and conditions of employment including dismissal provisions, holidays, various condition allowances etc. for a period of 2 years in most cases. Wage agreements normally contain an index-linking clause; the rates they fix are in principle minima, but in view of the importance of individual companies in the largest sectors, such rates frequently acquire a standard character.

Staff employees are represented by a separate union in collective bargaining, and in general legislation, agreements and practice treat them separately. They have, however, negotiated since 1965, and in manufacturing staff employees are around 80% organised (manual workers: 50%). Additionally, there are signs that the two categories will gradually be aligned — largely under the influence of their French and Dutch neighbours.

Conditions of employment

Remuneration.

The real increase in wages in Luxembourg between 1964 and 1971 was the lowest in the Community: 28%. Annual rates of increase over the last few years have been relatively high, however, as consumer prices have risen much more slowly than in other parts of Europe. (For differentials between the various branches of industry, see Appendix (ii), p.110.) Manual workers are normally paid a standard time rate, which may or may not be accompanied by efficiency bonuses: these, however, are declining in importance.

Hours of work

The legal maximum is 48 hours for manual workers and 44 for non-manual. The 40-hour week will be introduced within 5-10 years. Agreements reduce these hours to 41-44 for manual workers, and 40 for non-manual workers. Overtime is paid at an additional 25% by law, in practice 30% for the first four hours and 50% thereafter.

Annual holidays

The holiday entitlement is 17-22 days according to age (increased entitlement at age 30 and 38). They are paid at average earnings: in some cases additional holiday pay is agreed domestically.

Public holidays

There are 10 paid public holidays:

New Year's Day	Assumption Day
Easter Monday	All Saints Day
May Day	Christmas Day
Ascension Day	Boxing Day
Whit Monday	National holiday (23rd June)

Employee representation

Employee Delegates

Representative bodies for manual workers (up to 20 members) and staff workers (3 or more members according to the size of the undertaking) must be set up in plants employing more than 15 manual and more than 12 staff employees respectively. Election is based on trade union nominations. The Delegates represent individuals in disputes, participate in the organisation of training and welfare facilities and must be consulted on matters affecting the Works Rules, and on plant wage classifications and bonuses if provision for this is expressly made in collective agreements. The Delegates also have to be informed in cases of summary dismissals.

Recent developments

Recent Parliamentary Bills have envisaged employee representation on Supervisory Boards (conseil d'administration), and the subject has been discussed at length in the tripartite Economic and Social Council. One of the main objections has been that such a development would not encourage the continued foreign investment — particularly of US companies — on which Luxembourg has come to rely to a considerable extent. Union leadership is now somewhat divided on the question, with the result that it will not be further considered for the moment. Instead, the unions are concentrating on proposals for joint works councils, and increased union access to the plant.

Total Labour Cost — E.E.C. breakdown for 1969

Manual Workers	%
1. Direct wages and regular bonuses	69.64
2. Other bonuses and *ex gratia* payments	2.97
3. Payment for days not worked (holidays etc)	9.65
4. Employers' social security contributions	
— sickness, disability, maternity, retirement, unemployment	7.56
— industrial accidents and diseases	3.44
— family allowances	3.23
— other statutory contributions	0.01
TOTAL, statutory contributions	14.24
— company or sector insurance schemes	0.00
— supplementary retirement pensions	0.02
— contractual or voluntary wage and salary guarantee	0.00
— supplementary unemployment insurance	—
— contractual supplementary family allowances	0.43
— other contractual or voluntary payments	0.01
TOTAL, contractual and voluntary payments	0.47
TOTAL, employer contributions to social security	14.70
5. Payments in kind	0.97
6. Other payments of a social nature	1.52
7. Training costs	0.55
8. Social taxes	—
TOTAL LABOUR COST	100.00

Total Labour Cost — E.E.C. breakdown for 1969

Staff Employees	%
1. Direct wages and regular bonuses	63.32
2. Other bonuses and *ex gratia* payments	7.68
3. Payment for days not worked (holidays etc)	11.61
4. Employers' social security contributions	
— sickness, disability, maternity, retirement, unemployment	5.35
— industrial accidents and diseases	1.81
— family allowances	1.49
— other statutory contributions	0.06
TOTAL, statutory contributions	8.70
— company or sector insurance schemes	0.03
— supplementary retirement pensions	2.40
— contractual or voluntary wage and salary guarantee	0.00
— supplementary unemployment insurance	
— contractual supplementary family allowances	0.25
— other contractual or voluntary payments	0.68
TOTAL, contractual and voluntary payments	3.36
TOTAL, employer contributions to social security	12.06
5. Payments in kind	3.34
6. Other payments of a social nature	1.87
7. Training costs	0.12
8. Social taxes	—
TOTAL LABOUR COST	**100.00**

7. Denmark

Employment

Recruitment

There are no regulations governing recruitment.

Contract of employment

Form. The contract must be written.

Duration. Contracts are generally of indefinite duration.

Content. The individual contract contains the main terms of employment, including the relevant provisions of collective agreements or laws (in the case of staff employees) and the individual rate of pay.

Termination — dismissals — redundancy

The contract may be terminated by notice. Notice given by the manual employee is 7 days after 1 year's service, and 10 days after 5 years' service. Staff employees must give 1 month's notice. Periods of notice to be respected by the employer for manual employees vary slightly according to sector. The most usual are:

Manual workers	
1 year's service	14 days
3 years' service	28 days
5 years' service	35 days
8 years' service	56 days
Staff employees (regulated by law)	
up to 6 months' service	1 month
6 months — 3 years.	3 months

3 years – 6 years	4 months
6 years – 9 years	5 months
9 years and above	6 months

Dismissals. Dismissals may be made with notice or summarily without notice for a 'just cause'. There is no provision for severance pay. Shop stewards are protected from dismissal except for 'just cause'.

Redundancy. Shop stewards must be informed in advance of planned dismissals, whether individual or collective.

Industrial relations

Denmark's system of industrial relations bears a marked resemblance to the United Kingdom's traditional system: Government intervention is minimal and restricted to crises; wages and conditions are negotiated at national level voluntarily, and represent minima; actual wage levels are settled at plant-level. There is also a long tradition of shop stewards, who represent unions which in the main are organised along craft lines, although, as in UK, the number of unions is being encouraged to diminish in favour of larger, more 'industrial' or 'general' unions. There are, however, some significant differences, and most of these derive from the fact that Denmark's total population is only 5 million. Strong centralisation, subject to extensive participation from individuals, is in the interests of both unions and employers, between whose organisations there is a basis of co-operation such that the role of the Government is minimal.

Trade unions

About two-thirds of Denmark's 1.8 million wage and salary earners belong to trade unions: in industry, manual workers are practically 100% organised, while office staffworker unionization within LO is around 50%.

LO (Landsorganisationen i Danmark/Danish Federation of Trade Unions) is the most important trade union body: through its 50 member unions, it represents some 900,000 workers (of whom 28% are women). In the main, LO's member unions recruit on a craft basis – including unions for unskilled men and unskilled women. These national unions consist of a large number of locals (3000), and Denmark has a highly developed shop steward tradition at plant-level.

Outside LO, about 250,000 belong to civil service unions, and unions for professional and managerial staff: for industry, the most important of the latter is Faellesrepraesentationen (The Common Representation), which has an agreement with DAF on certain wage items but otherwise is subject to the terms and conditions of employment laid down in legislation. Non-LO unions are relatively unimportant.

Employers' associations

Associations for the individual branches of industry belong to the DAF (Dansk Arbeidsgivereforening/Danish Employers' Confederation), which is the bargaining partner of the LO.

Collective bargaining

Wage rates, and all other conditions of employment are regulated in 2-year agreements between DAF and LO for both manual and non-manual employees. Co-ordinated agreements are simultaneously concluded for individual branches of industry. These set out minimum rates for the various categories of workers (e.g. skilled, semi-skilled and unskilled male and female) and include a cost-of-living escalator clause. General increases may also be made. Earnings, and individual rates, are left to be agreed between employee and employer at domestic level, with the proviso that questions relating to the cost-of-living may not be included in domestic wage-determination. The 1971 agreement includes provisions for equal pay to be discussed in the 1973 negotiations.

Legislation provides a procedure to be implemented when negotiations break down, and DAF and LO have agreed a precise timetable — with dates — for when they will refer the question. A State conciliation board attempts a mediated settlement, failing which industrial action may be taken. (LO rules forbid the rejection of a mediation proposal unless a majority of members have voted against, and the negative votes constitute 35% of those entitled to vote.) Where the state conciliator considers that industrial action (for which 2 weeks' notice is required) would endanger the nation's 'health or safety', he may order a cooling-off period of one month. Thereafter, the Government may intervene through Parliament, but not normally until the strike or lock-out has been effective for some time.

Disputes on the interpretation of an agreement go through a 3-

stage procedure before being referred to the Industrial Relations Court. Disputes are usually settled, however, at the domestic level.

Conditions of employment

Remuneration

From 1964 to 1971, real wages rose by 46%: this figure conceals rapid increases in wages and prices, both of which have increased faster than any other country in the Nine. There are signs, however, that the spiral has slowed down in the last two or three years.

Payment systems relate to the centrally-agreed minimum rates, and may take the form of straight timework, or piecework whose precise rates are the subject of domestic regulation. Personal bonuses may complete the wage, but their composition may be fairly arbitrary. While formal merit-rating schemes and job evaluation are rare, they have been the subject of joint discussions and may well be progressively introduced.

Hours of work

Standard hours of work are currently 41¾; 40 hours for 2nd and 3rd shift workers. The working week is 5 or 5½ days, according to domestic agreement. Average hours worked are currently about 43. Overtime is paid at fixed money rates, which are equivalent to approximately time-and-a-fifth for the first two hours, just over time-and-a-third for the 3rd and 4th hours, and almost time-and-three-quarters thereafter.

Annual holidays

The annual entitlement for 1972 is 3 weeks and 3 days (21 workable days): as from 1st April 1973, it will be 4 weeks (24 days). The holiday allowance is 9.5% of earnings in the year preceding the holiday.

Public holidays

There are 10½ public holidays in Denmark: all are paid except

May Day.

New Year's Day	Whit Monday
Maundy Thursday	Christmas Day
Good Friday	Boxing Day
Easter Monday	National holiday (5th June)
May Day (unpaid)	Repentance Day (½ day only)

Social security

Very little of Denmark's comprehensive social security system is paid for directly by employer and employee contributions. DAF and LO operate a supplementary pension system, but the Danish employer's contribution to social security still accounts for only about 2% of total labour cost.

Labour cost

There are no E.E.C. labour cost breakdown figures for Denmark, but a private estimate for 1968 — accurate to ± 1%, however — gives the following:

1. Direct wages incl. bonuses	88.8%
2. Payment for days not worked	9.2%
3. Social security contributions	2.0%
	100.0%

Employee representation

Shop stewards (Tillidsmand)

By agreement, shop stewards may be elected in establishments with more than 5 employees. Shop stewards are automatically members of the Works Council.

Stewards' functions are mainly those of representing their members' interests in disputes over wages and working conditions. The Danish shop steward system is the nearest to the UK situation.

Works Council

Under the terms of the 1970 DAF/LO agreement, establishments employing more than 50 are to set up joint works councils with 6-12 members according to the size of the plant, consisting of an equal number of employee and management representatives. The Works Council has rights of consultation and information on general personnel policy, work organization, and the financial situation of the company. It further discusses payment systems — with particular emphasis on increasing productivity — and training and social welfare funds. For this, it may set up subcommittees (e.g. work study committee etc.).

LO has developed claims for 'economic democracy' as a consistent policy. In addition to wage investment schemes, 'economic democracy' includes increased employee participation in the management of the enterprise. It is therefore possible that some form of co-determination on the Board may be sought, even if it does not take the advanced form of the German model.

8. Eire

Industrial relations

Many features of industrial relations in Eire derive from a close relationship with Britain. The most obvious is the traditional voluntarism and the unwillingness of Government to intervene in the collective bargaining process, to the extent that a Labour Ministry was set up as late as the mid-60s. Trade Union Acts of 1941 and 1971, and Industrial Relations Acts of 1946 and 1969 represent the main legislative incursions into this tradition; in the 60s, an Industrial Training Act and a Redundancy Payments Act were the major Government initiatives; and in 1970, when negotiations broke down, the Government threatened legislation on wages and prices. (It withdrew the Bill when agreement was reached.) The main legislation introduced only a limited framework for collective bargaining, and beyond this the bargaining partners negotiate at national and domestic level. The size of the country and its industrial concentrations have meant that the distinction between the various levels of negotiation is smaller than in most countries. Nevertheless, wages and conditions are agreed both at branch of industry level and individually for companies or plants, and in this respect there is some similarity with the UK. While there is no standard pattern of negotiation, bargaining tends to take place in 'wage rounds', which may last up to two years at a time: and there is a developing tendency for wage questions to be settled in outline between employers and unions as a whole before the branch of industry agreements are negotiated. The last two 'wage rounds', the 13th (1970) and the 14th (1972) have taken place within the loose and relatively informal framework of an employer/labour conference: and, among the developments which this either has brought or will bring to industrial relations in Eire, there has been an attempt to synchronize the duration of wage agreements, disputes procedures on interpretation (in some circumstances including reference to the Labour Court) have been set up, joint sub-committees of the conference have approached a number of questions, such as dismissals, fair employment codes, worker participation etc. and some thought has been given to expanding the range of subjects for national negotiation within the conference to include fringe benefits and other conditions of employment. The fact that the conference has survived considerable upheavals (especially during the 14th wage round) may be indicative of the direction in which Irish industrial relations are heading.

Trade unions

52% of the Irish labour force belong to trade unions. The more important unions are based in Eire, but British unions — mainly craft — have Irish sections which additionally affiliate to the ICTU. The situation is further complicated by the fact that many unions draw their membership from both sides of the border. (The bulk of UK labour legislation does not apply in Northern Ireland, however, where the question of industrial relations is under separate discussion.)

> ICTU (Irish Congress of Trade Unions): this confederation's member unions cover 90% of the organized workforce. The largest member is the ITGWU (Irish Transport and General Workers) which alone represents some 38% of ICTU's membership. There is a large number of small unions representing crafts, white-collar workers and civil servants.

There have been various attempts by the ICTU to rationalize the structure of unions, but these have been largely without success. Unions are organized on a branch basis: due to the small average size of an Irish plant, multi-union problems rarely arise at that level. But poaching is still a problem, especially as UK unions operating in Eire can offer their members larger financial benefits.

Employers' associations

The association representing the largest numbers employed by its member companies is the FUE (Federated Union of Employers), which has an exclusively industrial relations function. It covers private industry through 10 regional and 80 industrial branches. In 1970 a body known as IEC (Irish Employers' Confederation) was set up for industrial relations questions to include also members from State-owned companies and organisations. Because of its overall coverage, this body nominates employer representatives to the Labour Court, various tribunals (including those set up under the

1968 Redundancy Payments Act) and the employer/labour conference.

Collective bargaining

To engage in collective bargaining, unions and employers' associations must be licensed, which involves putting forward a deposit with the High Court. These provisions of the 1941 Act were strengthened in the 1971 Act, when 18 months' notice became necessary for an application for a bargaining licence; for a union, membership must be over 500, and the deposit stands at £5000.

Wages are negotiated initially, in the wage rounds, centrally by the employer/labour conference: thereafter, the branches of industry negotiate their own agreements along the lines laid down centrally. At present, other conditions and fringe benefits are not dealt with in the conference, but are settled either at branch level or domestically. Agreements are not normally held to be legally enforceable, although a feature of the 1970 and subsequent agreements was the introduction of an agreed embargo on industrial action during the currency of the agreements. There is also provision under the 1946 Act for agreements registered with the Labour Court to be declared binding on all employers in a particular area or sector (an 'extension' provision) on the application of one party and with the substantial consent of both. In this case, it must contain provision for a disputes procedure and an obligation to maintain industrial peace: and the agreement is held to be generally enforceable at law.

Labour Court

The Labour Court was set up under the 1946 Act, and consists of a chairman, a deputy chairman, and two members nominated by the ICTU and two from the IEC: all are Government appointments. The Court is supported by a number of conciliation officers, and the Court's function lies very largely in conciliation. When collective negotiations break down, the dispute may be referred to the Court, or it may initiate an investigation on its own initiative. It may then publish a recommendation, but has no power to enforce it. (In a very limited number of situations the Court may order a cooling-off period by imposing an award for three months: but this procedure has rarely been used.)

Rights Commissioners

Rights Commissioners have the authority to conduct an investigation of a dispute if it is referred to them by a party to the dispute, and no other party objects. The two Commissioners, however may not investigate disputes involving wages and conditions: their functions are limited to dismissals and demarcation questions etc.

Conditions of employment

Remuneration

Real wages rose by 43% between 1964 and 1971 — the third highest rate in the Community of Nine. Nevertheless, in money terms rates tend to be lower than in most other countries. The cost-of-living is commensurately lower. Wages are established at local or plant level on the basis of national minima. Payment systems are mainly timework and classical piecework.

Hours of work

A 40-hour, 5-day week is worked. Overtime is paid at a standard time and a half.

Holidays

The minimum annual holiday entitlement by law is 2 weeks including Sundays (i.e. 10 days). There are 5 additional days by agreement, making a total of 15 days. Public holidays, by law, are 6:

St. Patrick's Day (March 17th)	1st Monday in August
Easter Monday	Christmas Day
Whit Monday	Boxing Day

All holidays are paid at average earnings.

Appendices to Part 1.

Appendix (i)

Employment in the E.E.C. and Applicants

Mid-year 1970 or annual average 1970

	Total popu-lation millions	Civil labour force millions	Wage and salary earners millions	Unemploy-ment as % of civil work-force	Women as % of civil work-force	Labour force [1] in: Industry	Agric.	Services
Belgium	9.7	3.8	2.9	2.0	29	44	5	49
France	50.8	20.8	15.9	1.7	37	40	14	44
Germany	60.8	26.9	21.9	0.6	34	49	9	41
Italy	54.5	19.4	12.8	3.2	26	42	19	35
Luxembourg	0.3	0.1	0.1	0.0	26	47	11	42
Netherlands	13.0	4.6	3.8	1.2	23	41	7	51
Six	189.0	(75.6)	(57.4)	(1.7)	32	n.a.	n.a.	n.a.
UK	55.7	25.5	22.9	2.2	36	46	3	49
Norway	3.9	1.5	1.2[2]	1.5[2]	30[2]	36[2]	15[2]	48[2]
Denmark	4.9	2.3	1.8[2]	1.1[2]	37[2]	38[2]	12[2]	48[2]
Ireland (Rep.)	3.0	1.1	0.7	5.2[2]	27[2]	28	27	40

Source: ECSO, OECD   [1]Balance to 100% represents unemployed   [2]1969   n.a. = not available

109

Appendix (ii)

Table of average gross hourly wages in the most important branches of industry

(All industries = 100)

Branch of industry	Germany April 1964	Germany April 1970	France March 1964	France March 1970	Italy April 1964	Italy April 1970	Netherlands April 1964	Netherlands April 1970	Belgium April 1964	Belgium April 1970	Luxembourg April 1964	Luxembourg April 1970
Extraction of oil and natural gas	99.7	101.2	136.7	·	160.7	149.4	127.1	152.7	152.6	159.0	·	·
Oil industry	112.6	115.7	143.6	171.5	155.6	161.2	103.2	104.9	103.0	111.6	·	·
Printing and publishing	108.4	119.3	139.6	146.1	138.8	135.6	140.8	123.6	125.8	124.3	85.2	89.4
Coalmining	110.7	106.0	117.3	102.8	106.5	228.3	115.9	112.9	123.9	119.4	·	·
Ferrous and non-ferrous metals	111.0	110.7	103.8	105.1	119.1	126.1	105.8	102.3	116.9	115.4	108.4	118.8
Transport vehicles	109.7	111.9	114.2	114.2	123.3	121.3	100.4	99.8	108.7	105.4	79.1	69.0
Non-electrical machinery	103.4	104.6	111.0	111.1	106.7	111.8	104.7	111.9	102.5	111.5	60.1	82.4
Chemicals	101.3	103.9	111.6	118.1	103.4	116.1	·	·	·	·	·	69.8
Metal ores	102.1	102.0	152.9	134.2	130.1	106.3	·	·	·	·	112.7	121.3
Building	112.0	107.5	98.3	96.6	119.4	105.3	111.6	110.0	101.9	102.7	72.9	74.3
General average	100.0	100.0	100.0	100.0	100.0	100.0	100.0	100.0	100.0	100.0	100.0	100.0
Non-metallic mineral products	98.7	98.5	100.6	106.0	91.3	92.7	101.1	105.3	99.9	103.0	77.0	76.2
Metal products	98.4	98.3	98.8	98.8	87.6	98.7	98.2	98.9	104.6	99.0	83.4	76.1
Rubber, plastics, artificial and synthetic fibres	95.0	96.6	99.1	99.6	111.5	98.0	104.0	109.8	95.0	97.8	·	·
Electrical machinery and supplies	90.1	90.4	105.8	105.5	101.7	103.2	93.9	91.9	96.6	97.8	86.5	90.6
Beverages	93.7	97.3	95.7	98.4	98.9	96.8	99.3	101.3	90.1	93.5	78.0	76.3
Paper and paper goods	88.7	92.7	93.9	98.8	104.8	103.3	100.4	104.9	96.6	98.0	·	72.7
Wood and cork	87.0	89.1	86.1	87.6	75.3	72.2	93.1	91.9	87.1	90.6	58.2	59.9
Leather	84.8	85.8	85.5	84.4	83.1	77.5	84.5	83.7	80.1	82.4	·	·
Food industries (excluding fats and beverages)	80.9	83.8	88.4	91.8	98.9	93.0	90.6	96.2	86.5	86.2	65.6	68.4
Tobacco	73.3	82.2	·	·	80.1	107.5	86.3	86.4	75.8	85.3	58.4	67.1
Textiles	83.2	85.7	81.2	81.7	81.7	74.9	88.8	91.7	83.6	83.3	·	52.3
Footwear and clothing, bedding	76.7	76.3	83.5	83.7	72.5	66.9	64.6	67.5	68.0	72.5	42.5	45.4

Source: 'Statistiques harmonisées des gains horaires bruts des ouvriers dans l'industrie', Social Statistics, No.5 - 1970, Statistical Office of the European Communities.

Table of average gross hourly wages of industry by regions

(Whole country = 100)

GERMANY — Land	April 1964	April 1970
Hamburg	112.8	112.1
North-Rhine/Westphalia	106.0	104.9
Bremen	104.5	103.4
Lower Saxony	100.8	101.2
Hessen	100.7	101.0
Schleswig-Holstein	101.5	100.5
Saar	102.1	99.0
Berlin	94.0	100.8
Baden-Württemberg	95.8	98.1
Rhineland-Palatinate	95.9	95.1
Bavaria	90.2	90.8
FRANCE (1) — Region	**March 1964**	**March 1970**
Paris (City)	120.8	116.6
Mediterranean	98.8	100.9
Rhone Valley	98.0	97.9
Paris region	94.4	96.1
East	93.9	95.1
North	91.2	91.0
Massif Central	91.2	90.6
West	89.2	90.5
Aquitaine region	87.7	92.1
ITALY — Region	**April 1964**	**October 1969**
Liguria	115.5	113.4
Piedmont — Val d'Aosta	111.1	109.9
Latium	104.1	104.7
Lombardy	99.1	101.0
Tuscany-Umbria	94.9	96.7
Sicily-Sardinia	95.9	95.3
Emilia Romagna-Marches	91.6	96.1
Venice region	92.4	92.6
Campania	97.9	89.3
Other regions of Southern Italy	86.2	93.4
NETHERLANDS — Region	**April 1964**	**April 1970**
North and South Holland, Utrecht	103.6	106.4
Other provinces	97.5	96.8

Source: 'Statistiques harmonisees des gains horaires bruts des ouvriers de l'industrie'. Statistical Office of the European Communities.
(1) Manufacturing industries only.

Appendix (iv)

Total Labour Cost — breakdown for 1969

Manual workers	Germany [1]	France [1]	Italy [1]	Belgium [1]	Nether-lands [1]	Luxem-bourg [1]	Norway [2]	U.K. [3]
1. Direct wages and regular bonuses	69.19	60.23	52.66	63.43	61.75	69.64	}75.67	}83.90
2. Other bonuses and *ex gratia* payments	2.88	2.44	7.05	2.54	2.77	2.97		
3. Payment for days not worked	10.31	8.35	8.25	11.01	10.68	9.65	10.28	7.30
4. Employers social security contributions								
— *sickness, disability, maternity, retirement, unemployment*	*11.02*	*11.30*	*19.60*	*10.35*	}*11.01*	*7.56*		
— *industrial accidents and diseases*	*1.81*	*3.16*	*2.34*	*2.93*		*3.44*		
— *family allowances (State)*	*–*	*7.31*	*6.12*	*6.51*	*3.93*	*3.23*		
— *other legal contributions*	*0.02*	*0.33*	*0.30*	*0.89*	*–*	*0.01*		
TOTAL statutory contributions	*12.84*	*22.11*	*28.37*	*20.68*	*14.94*	*14.24*		
— *company or sector insurance schemes*	*0.02*	*0.20*	*0.29*	*0.05*	*0.69*	*0.00*		
— *supplementary retirement pensions*	*1.39*	*2.01*	*0.16*	*0.20*	*3.13*	*0.02*		
— *contractual/voluntary wage guarantee*	*0.05*	*0.18*	*–*	*0.06*	*0.49*	*0.00*		
— *suppl. unemployment insurance*	*–*	*0.23*	*–*	*–*	*–*	*–*		
— *contractual suppl. family allowances*	*0.25*	*0.09*	*0.03*	*0.04*	*0.09*	*0.43*		
— *other contractual or voluntary payments*	*0.05*	*0.15*	*0.09*	*0.08*	*0.07*	*0.01*		
TOTAL contractual and voluntary payments	*1.76*	*2.86*	*0.57*	*0.43*	*4.46*	*0.47*		
TOTAL, employer s.s. contributions	14.61	24.97	28.94	21.11	19.40	14.70	11.04	6.50
5. Payments in kind	0.67	1.63	0.18	0.41	0.46	0.97	0.07	0.10
6. Other payments of a social nature	–	–	1.25	–	–	–	–	–
7. Training costs	1.38	1.61	1.20	1.22	3.66	1.52	2.49	}2.20
8. Social taxes	0.96	0.76	0.47	0.28	1.27	0.55	0.45	
GRAND TOTAL	100.00	100.00	100.00	100.00	100.00	100.00	100.00	100.00

Non-manual workers

	Germany [1]	France [1]	Italy [1]	Belgium [1]	Netherlands [1]	Luxembourg [1]	Norway [2]	U.K.
1. Direct wages and regular bonuses	72.51	62.19	55.87	63.30	60.18	63.32	} 72.48	*not available*
2. Other bonuses and ex gratia payments	–	5.02	7.76	7.57	6.89	7.68		
3. Payment for days not worked	9.91	8.07	10.60	12.04	10.88	11.61	10.00	
4. Employers social security contributions								
– *sickness, disability, maternity, retirement, unemployment*	*8.33*	*8.33*	*18.73*	*6.12*	} *7.36*	*5.35*		
– *industrial accidents and diseases*	*1.00*	*1.69*	*0.68*	*1.25*		*1.81*		
– *family allowances (State)*	–	*5.13*	*3.66*	*4.92*	*3.36*	*1.49*		
– *other legal contributions*	*0.02*	*0.14*	*0.39*	*0.08*	–	*0.06*		
TOTAL statutory contributions	*9.34*	*15.30*	*23.46*	*12.37*	*10.99*	*8.70*		
– *company or sector insurance schemes*	*0.18*	*0.21*	*0.27*	*3.37*	*0.75*	*0.03*		
– *suppl. retirement pensions*	*4.76*	*4.46*	*0.14*	–	*6.48*	*2.40*		
– *contractual/voluntary wage guarantee*	*0.06*	*0.34*	–	–	*0.43*	*0.00*		
– *suppl. unemployment insurance*	–	*0.24*	–	–	–	–		
– *contractual suppl. family allowances*	*0.32*	*0.09*	*0.02*	–	*0.06*	*0.25*		
– *other contractual or voluntary payments*	*0.06*	*0.20*	*0.14*	–	*0.06*	*0.68*		
TOTAL contractual and voluntary payments	*5.38*	*5.54*	*0.56*	*3.37*	*7.79*	*3.36*		
TOTAL, employer s.s. contributions	14.72	20.84	24.03	15.74	18.78	12.06	14.78	
5. Payments in kind	0.52	1.49	0.18	0.48	0.48	3.34	0.07	
6. Other payments of a social nature	1.34	1.70	0.86	0.74	2.34	1.87	2.17	
7. Training costs	1.00	0.69	0.22	0.12	0.45	0.12	0.50	
8. Social taxes	–	–	0.49	–	–	–	–	
GRAND TOTAL	100.00	100.00	100.00	100.00	100.00	100.00	100.00	

1) E.E.C. labour cost survey for 1969   2) private estimate, based on Norwegian figures for 1969
3) Department of Employment estimate: figures for staff n.a.

Part 2. The European Communities

9. The social policies of the European Communities

The 1957 Treaty of Rome contains a number of Articles relating to 'social provisions' — that is, employment and industrial relations — of which probably the best-known and at the same time least significant are those concerning free movement of labour and equal pay for women.

The original signatories attached some importance to these provisions, which were included for not entirely economic reasons; the opening lines of the Treaty refer to 'an accelerated raising of the standard of living', and in the first Article of those which relate directly to social provisions (117 - 122) they agree "upon the need to promote better conditions of living and of work and employment for workers, so as to lead to the equalisation of such conditions in an upward direction'. (The last two words are important) Yet, as will be seen, the social provisions of the 1957 Treaty are a fairly mixed bag, with explicit and detailed reference to equal pay in an Article only a few words shorter than the one which covers everything from labour law and collective bargaining to occupational diseases and social security. In short, the Treaty expediently left the door open for further developments later and tied up a few urgent loose ends. It was not until after 1958, and the advent of a more social-democrat Commission, that the Communities began to look at all closely at the question of manpower and employment policies, and at the harmonisation of factors affecting employment and industrial relations.

In the late 60s, the Community began to integrate its various elements: the three Treaties — E.E.C., Coal and Steel, Euratom — were placed under the supervision of a single Commission, who now set about transforming an effective customs union into a genuine common market. To do this, it was clear that the Community would have to go beyond the mere monitoring of the implementation of the original Treaties and the somewhat piecemeal approach to crises. It was necessary to devise a set of co-ordinated, constructive policies in various fields — economic, monetary, industrial, regional — which overlap and influence each other. The development of such policies is not, as such, an explicit Treaty obligation. But its necessity is implied, both in order to attain the basic objectives of the E.E.C. Treaty, and in order to face the broader problems of a more political approach to European integration. The range of co-ordinated policies must, of course, take into account questions of employment and industrial relations; and the Commission has now begun to investigate seriously the areas of possible harmonization outlined in Article 118 of the 1957 Treaty. As yet the plans are tentative, but certain concrete steps have already been taken.

Firstly, when the Commission and High Authorities were merged, a number of residual funds came under the control of the single Commission, together with the existing E.E.C. Social Fund — all of which were designed for use in training and retraining schemes in declining or developing industries. The Social Fund has been reformed (its scope has been widened) and the Commission proposes to use it in the context of the co-ordinated policies.

Secondly, the Commission has proposed a statute for 'European companies' — i.e. those operating within two or more Community States — which would be separate from existing national company legislation. Because of the diverse nature of company laws in the Six, and in particular because of the differing degrees of worker representation on the Boards and in the management of companies in individual countries, the Commission has found it impossible to exclude a number of proposals on worker — or trade union — involvement in its proposed statute. Quite apart from the implications in terms of 'upwards harmonization', this question has produced the first major European row in industrial relations.

Thirdly, the Commission has begun its consultations on a full-scale 'co-ordinated', social policy. At the time of writing this has progressed no further than a set of draft policy guidelines. But its proposals on the development of manpower and employment policies will be of great significance — not least to the UK's own declining industries and development areas — and the total package already shows that the Community is preparing to devote considerably more attention to 'social affairs' than hitherto, both by expanding the provisions of the Treaty of Rome and by going beyond them in co-ordination with the other major policies.

Whether the Commission will continue to develop the policies and — of importance to the future of all of them — whether monetary union can be achieved by the end of the decade, depends largely on the effect of entry of the three new members (and one of them in particular). If their approach is not conflicting, and there is some evidence that recent policies within the United Kingdom have been designed to connect with the E.E.C. approach, then progress on social policy will be rapid and, for some, not very comfortable.

Competition and harmonization

It was one of the aims of the original Treaty to improve the living and working conditions of Community nationals and to spread the benefits deriving from intra-E.E.C. trade as widely as possible among those living in the member States — just as the Treaty also aimed to give material and technical assistance to developing countries outside the Six. But these broad principles are not the sole, and in some ways not the major consideration which needs to be kept in mind when looking at the development of the E.E.C.'s social policy.

The intention of 'harmonization' or 'equalization' is to establish a common market where, when national tariffs have been removed, competition is not distorted by reason of one country having an unfair competitive advantage over another. In order to identify such competitive imbalances, and to eliminate them, the E.E.C. is logically bound to investigate all the factors which bear on the relative competitiveness of the different countries. Production costs are a major area. The Community has of course spent a lot of time on raw materials pricing, transport, uniform service-based taxation accounting etc.; but it is increasingly applying itself to other areas of cost. The most sizeable outstanding item to which the Commission must apply itself is that of the cost which an employer must incur, by reason of national legislation or collective agreements, from employing workers.

All other things being equal, this can logically be interpreted as meaning that the E.E.C. ultimately aims to produce standard rates of pay and conditions throughout Europe. At the moment, however, all other things are obviously *not* equal. Many hidden elements, deriving from differing taxation systems, differing methods of financing social security, different labour market conditions even within the Six member States, distort any attempt at a realistic comparison of the cost of employing a worker.

'Harmonization' has, in the past, been able to mean compatibility rather than comparability. This was particularly the case where broad generalisations were being made; for example, the question was not so much 'how do the supplementary pension benefits compare as between countries' as 'do such systems exist in all countries'. Because of the make-up of labour cost in various countries, no uniform system for any single factor could be introduced without the risk of increasing competitive imbalances rather than diminishing them: and the details of such matters still differ widely. The Community has proceeded, and must continue to proceed, with caution; it must also rely on co-operation rather than instruction which it could not enforce.

It cannot be stressed too strongly that the Commission is not going to issue directions with which every individual company is going to have to comply. Major problems of harmonization at Government level have to be dealt with first. So far, the Commission has tended not to take the initiative but simply to collaborate when national Governments have put forward new proposals.

In the past few years, industrial relations systems in Europe have not stood still. Other European countries have gone through as much legislative and contractual activity as the United Kingdom, and in general national solutions have been sought for national problems. What makes the Commission's job easier is the fact that as a result of a more European outlook — itself encouraged by the internationalisation of industry and commerce — a good deal of cross-fertilization of ideas has taken place both at Government level and in terms of the kind of claims which are being raised by national unions. This has been reflected in international activities of unions (and employers), and it is clear that any harmonization of industrial relations system will henceforth be subject to considerably more institutionalised and informal lobbying than has been the case up to now. But the Commission would probably be the first to accept that if harmonization could come about through national or international agreement, that would be no bad thing; and the social policy guidelines show that their thinking is tending in that direction.

10. Provisions of the Treaty of Rome

Free movement of labour

Articles 48 and 49 guarantee the freedom of nationals of an E.E.C. member country to work in any other member State without discrimination on the grounds of nationality. But the Treaty specified that this was dependent on 'offers of employment actually made'; which, in the terms of Regulation 38/64 meant that a worker had to accept an offer made through a national employment agency in his home country in order to be free to move. Work and residence permits were dependent on such an offer.

Since 1st July 1968, however, these requirements have been relaxed. E.E.C. nationals may accept offers of employment on equal terms with nationals of the other country. On production of passport or identity card, a 'Residence Permit of a National of an E.E.C. Member State' is issued, valid for 5 years and renewable. The worker must still comply with public health and public safety requirements of the host country (in most cases these can be summarised as: no TB/VD, no criminal record).

In fact, the provisions on free movement within the Community have mainly been beneficial for Italian workers. The number of E.E.C. nationals working in the E.E.C. outside their own country is far outweighed by workers from non-E.E.C. countries — traditional labour markets are still of great importance (see p.122).

Under *Article 51*, social security benefits are to be made payable to migrant workers from other E.E.C. countries: and rights to such benefits should be transferable from one country to the next. Owing to the wide variety of systems in member States and differences in the risks covered, this has been a difficult Article to fulfil. The relevant provisions, however, have been made under Regulation 1408/71.

Foreign workers employed in the Community

Year	Belgium	Germany	France	Italy	Luxembourg	Netherlands	Community
1968: All	200,000	1,040,000	1,158,000	33,100	28,600	100,000	2,560,000
of which E.E.C.	123,000	380,000	262,400	10,000	24,700	43,000	843,000
1969: All	201,000	1,372,000	1,180,000	35,000	30,100	103,000	2,921,000
of which E.E.C.	123,000	427,000	260,000	11,000	25,200	45,000	891,000
1970: All	208,000	1,839,000	1,200,000	37,000	32,000	110,000	3,426,000
of which E.E.C.	125,000	478,000	260,000	12,000	26,000	50,000	951,000

Source: E.E.C.

The 'social provisions'

Article 117 states:

'Member States agree upon the need to promote better conditions of living and of work and employment for workers, so as to permit the equalisation of such conditions in an upward direction. They believe that such a development will ensue not only from the operation of the common market, which will favour the harmonization of social systems, but also from the procedures provided for in this Treaty and from the approximation of provisions imposed by law, regulation and administrative action'.

This Article, together with Article 118, gives an idea of the directions in which the Community is generally heading: but so far, little has been achieved among the precise objectives laid down in *Article 118:*

'Without prejudice to the other provisions of this Treaty and in conformity with its general objectives, the Commission shall have as its task the promotion of close collaboration between Member States in the social field, particularly in matters relating to:

- employment
- labour law and working conditions
- basic and advanced vocational training
- social security
- protection against occupational accidents and diseases
- occupational hygiene
- the law of trade unions, and collective bargaining between employers and workers

To this end the Commission shall act in close contact with Member States through the carrying out of studies, the giving of opinions and the organising of consultations both on problems arising at the national level and on those of concern to international organisations.'

(The Article adds that the Economic and Social Committee must be consulted before opinions are given.)

Most of the detailed list above has been left in abeyance for a considerable time: inevitably, any action requiring Community co-operation can only come about if the Member States see a need for it and have the will to collaborate. Vocational training, for example, is supported by Article 128 which proposes the establishment of general principles for a common policy on vocational training, but France and Germany have not been over-enthusiastic. Equally, the Commission has not taken a strong leading role in these areas, on the principle that Article 117 anticipated that these things would happen as a result of the functioning of the E.E.C.

Under the last Commission's approach to Europe's problems through co-ordinated policies, the matters listed in Article 118 have taken on a new significance.

Equal pay (Article 119)

'Each Member State shall . . . maintain the application of the principle of equal remuneration for the same work as between male and female workers.

For the purpose of this Article, remuneration shall be taken to mean the ordinary basic or minimum wage or salary, and any additional emoluments whatsoever payable directly or indirectly, whether in cash or in kind, by the employer to the worker and arising out of the worker's employment.

Equal remuneration without discrimination based on sex means:

a) that remuneration for the same work at piece rates shall be calculated on the basis of the same unit of measurement;
b) that remuneration for work at time-rates shall be the same for the same job.'

The Commission has issued five reports on the implementation of this Article between 1961 and 1970: the tenor of each was to note that some progress had been made, but that earnings differentials suggested that the provisions of the Article were not being fulfilled. The differentials probably arise from job grading systems — where, for example, physical criteria and the fact that women tend to be unskilled automatically downgrade them — and the fact that legislation in various countries protects women workers and thereby reduces their earnings potential. The terms of the UK Equal Pay Act are more stringent than Article 119; particularly in view of Britain's large number of employed women, this may induce the Commission to take stronger measures to implement Article 119, if the UK is not to be left at a competitive disadvantage.

The Social Fund

Articles 123-128 establish a social fund whose aim is to increase employment facilities and 'the geographical and occupational mobility of workers within the Community'. This was to be achieved by subsidising 50% of the cost of State schemes for

'a)   ensuring productive re-employment of workers by means of:
      — vocational re-training,
      — re-settlement allowances;
 b)   granting aid to workers whose employment is reduced or temporarily suspended, whether wholly or partly, as a result of the conversion of an undertaking to other production, in order that they may maintain the same wage-level pending their full re-employment.'

Up to the end of 1970, about $154 million had been paid out for the re-training and re-settlement of a million and a quarter workers. Within the next few years, however, the Commission sees the need for much more substantial sums, as a result of current trends of rationalisation and technological change, and also in view of the more active role it proposes to take on a variety of subjects through the new co-ordinated policies. For this reason, the Fund has been reformed, and from 1972 will operate on a budget of $37 million annually, rising over the next few years to $250 million per annum, which will be more widely available than under the old Fund. The new Fund will also be more flexible, and will help to compensate industries and regions which suffer as a result of Community policies; will help not only Government schemes but also those of nationalised and private industry acting 'in the public good' by up to 50% of the cost incurred; and may well be used for assistance during major industrial reorganisation or restructuring carried out by national bodies or the Community.

11. The European Company

The Commission submitted a draft statute for a 'European Company' (or 'SE — Societas Europea') to the Council in mid-1970; since that time, consultations have been underway, and there seems little likelihood of it being adopted by the Council before 1974. In the meantime it has aroused considerable opposition from many quarters, and most of them relate to the provisions for employee representation and influence in the SE, which are far-reaching.

The SE would stand as a piece of Community law, outside the jurisdiction of national company law, providing a legal status for companies operating in several Community countries, and there are overriding financial and commercial arguments for this. But the concept of a 'company' differs widely as between different national legislations, and the major problem was to establish which to use as a model. Finally, the two-tier Board model was chosen, not least because such a structure is already in operation in Germany, is optional for joint stock companies in France, is about to come into effect in the Netherlands and Norway, and is under consideration in Belgium and Luxembourg. In all these systems, employee representatives have some status on one of the Boards — the Supervisory one, but this varies from an advisory, non-voting role in France to the 50-50 control in the German coal and steel industries. The principle of 'upwards harmonization' then took concrete form; not surprisingly, the German unions are unwilling to surrender at European level rights which they have achieved at home, and the SE draft recognises this by proposing a two-thirds shareholder/one-third employee representation on the Supervisory Board of the SE. This has met with strong opposition from three quarters: from UNICE, the central employers' organization in the E.E.C., on principle; from the European unions (such as the European Metalworkers' Federation) who want one-third shareholders/one-third employees/one-third 'public interest' representation; and from certain unions in the E.E.C. notably the French and the Italians (and especially the Franco-Italian Communist group, CGT-CGIL) who oppose all forms of co-operation within capitalist systems on principle. The draft statute therefore permits employees *not* to be represented on the Supervisory Board if two-thirds of them so decide.

The SE draft statute also proposes a European Works Council;

members would be elected by each establishment according to the size of its labour force. The European Works Council would have information rights on financial and economic matters; consultation rights on a number of questions, and co-decision rights on:

'— rules relating to recruitment, promotion and dismissal of employees
— implementation of vocational training
— fixing of terms of remuneration and introduction of new methods of computing remuneration (this does not apply to individual questions)
— measures relating to industrial safety, health and hygiene
— introduction and management of social facilities
— daily time of commencement and termination of work
— preparation of the holiday schedule'
(Article 123 of the draft SE statute)

Cases of disagreement would be subject to an arbitration committee's ruling, made up of employer and employee members and a neutral chairman — the same institution as the conciliation committee under the 1972 Works Constitution Act in Germany.

Not the least significant of the Commission's proposals for the SE is that it shall have the right to make European collective agreements with trade unions or with the European Works Council, thereby by-passing national collective bargaining arrangements.

12. The social policy guidelines and the co-ordinated policies

The Commission's activities in the field of social policy got under way in 1970 with a major conference on employment and a decision in principle by the Council (in the shape of Labour and Social Affairs Ministers) to increase collaboration in this area. In 1971, the E.E.C. Social Affairs Commissioner, M. Coppé, published a set of 'preliminary guidelines for a social policy programme' which range over a very wide field, from housing, environmental pollution and general motivation of workers in a new technological society to detailed problems of declining industries, retraining and unemployment (*via*, it may be said, greater social justice and fairer distribution of wealth.) The Guidelines, which are in the nature of a consultative document have now been approved by the European Parliament; and they are evidence of the increasing awareness of the need for a Community-wide policy which will complete the package already largely worked out covering industrial policy, regional policy etc. The Commission draws the conclusion that the following items require priority action by the Community:

1. *Speedier achievement of the common labour market* through the development of active employment and manpower policies, through the removal of barriers which still exist and prevent complete freedom of movement; by integrating employment services' information.
2. *Absorption of under-employment and structural unemployment* by concentrating the Community's financial resources in co-operation with the regional policy (this includes a large increase in training facilities).
3. *Improvement of safety and health conditions at work and outside.*
4. *Improvement of women's working conditions.*
5. *Integration of handicapped persons into active life.*
6. *A social budget* should be drawn up at Community level covering all expenditure and provision of the necessary funds over a medium-term period.
7. *Collaboration between employers and employees.* The Commission recommends increasing the number of joint committees in all sectors and branches of the economy. It also proposes to increase its own

consultations with employers' and employees' organisations and suggests the development of European collective agreements, or model agreements on which national agreements can be based; the harmonisation of legislation on industrial relations, and the compilation of a European index of collective agreements.

When the Commission refers to 'European collective agreements' it is clearly thinking of standard wages and conditions in the long run, as is made clear in the SE draft statute. But it is realistic enough to be aware that such trends are unlikely in the short term. At the moment, the Commission is thinking in terms of, for example, harmonized dismissal and redundancy entitlements agreed for a sector of industry. (Its plans for *legislation* on harmonized dismissals entitlements have come up against strong German and UK opposition.) European sector agreements on such matters would fit more neatly into the Commission's plans, and might be practicable (as well as preferable). But the development of European collective agreements on substantive matters would need to be slow – they involve too many imponderables, quite apart from the unreality of setting up this kind of bargaining structure when it would have to include a country such as the UK. To conform to the Commission's present thinking, the UK would need to do several things to its industrial relations – from which, arguably, it could benefit in any case. These would include a much tighter control on who negotiates what at which level – preferably bolstered by agreed *and generally accepted* principles for matters such as job evaluation, work measurement and the establishment of piecerates; a formalisation of worker representation in the plant, which would inevitably involve the concession by employers of numerous managerial rights on a variety of subjects; and a number of other reforms all of which, in the British context, must be regarded as belonging to cloud-cuckoo-land, and the lack of which, in this country and in Italy in particular, may make the Commission's intentions difficult to put into effect, without adding a further dimension of chaos to a presently uneasy situation.

It is not clear when or whether these questions will be regulated along the lines so far put forward by the Commission, but there is no doubt that the UK will be considerably involved in formulating their final shape. In the months preceding the enlargement of the E.E.C., it was obvious that the Commission and their staff were at pains to get their complementary policies on 'social affairs' into public, if only draft form, before British entry. Thus the two-tier board structure has now appeared in the draft Fifth Directive on the harmonization of national company legislations: and proposals for harmonization of dismissals and redundancy practices in individual E.E.C. member States by a Directive were 'leaked'. In November, however, it was agreed that, in general, discussion on such questions would be postponed until after 1st January 1973. Thereafter, with full British participation, it will be difficult for the Community to press ahead with plans designed to harmonize the situation in the Six, unless the new marriage is intended to be purely morganatic. The tempo of activities in the Nine, however, can be expected to be as fast as it was in the last year of the Six, and the kind of question which may arise as a result of including the British situation in the policies which have so far been under consideration in the E.E.C. will be looked at in the section on the effect on the UK.

13. General European trends

It was mentioned earlier that the existence of the E.E.C. had led, quite independently of the institutions of the Community, to a cross-fertilization of ideas and claims in different countries. This effect is not limited to the member States of the Six or the Nine, but applies throughout western Europe, largely as a result of the interaction of a political entity (the E.E.C.) on linguistically and culturally connected groups of countries, some of which are in the E.E.C. while the rest remain outside.

The upheavals which spread through Europe in 1968 cannot entirely be attributed to sunspots; they also give some indication of this kind of interaction. Similarly, certain general trends in industrial relations can be observed which cannot by any means be ascribed merely to a growing economic interdependence.

a) Differentials are narrowing between the lowest paid and the highest paid.

b) Indirect wages and fringe benefits are making up an increasingly large proportion of total remuneration. (UK has not so far shown signs of this trend.) Total labour costs, insofar as they can be accurately estimated, show a surprisingly similar level in money terms.

c) Forms of saving/wage investment/profitsharing schemes are becoming prevalent, frequently associated with the performance of the company.

d) Staff employee, and managerial staff unionization is growing steadily.

e) There is a tendency for increased bargaining at plant level: this varies from the 'permanent negotiation' situation prevailing in Italy to the systems, as in Germany, where the subjects of such bargaining are clearly defined.

f) There is a large movement towards establishing a single status for manual workers and staff employees (which may explain d). This can be found in the Netherlands, in France, and in Switzerland; it has been claimed by Italian unions since 1963; it is commended in the UK Code of Practice; and German legislation has now removed practically all obstacles in its way.

g) Interest in achieving 'industrial democracy' has appeared in two main forms. Union access to the plant is now fairly generally provided for; and there has been much development of institutional committees with increased influence in areas which have traditionally been management's prerogative. (Certain *de facto* situations in British plants amount to the same thing.) Company legislation in several countries has given employee representatives a say in the overall running of the firm, and there is a marked tendency for employees' interests to be regarded as equally important as those of shareholders. This may well be further encouraged with the development of the holding company, whose involvement with the undertaking and the product is rather less than that of the traditional owner/employer. Secondly, and particularly in the Scandinavian countries, experiments in job enrichment techniques have had some effect in changing traditional workplace relationships. Labour disputes have become more aggressive. Both employers and workers have become more militant. While it is true that the countries granting their workers the fewest *rights* of influence have been hardest and most continuously hit, it is also true that underlying social, political and economic instability has probably contributed as much as any 'reactionary' employer outlook.

14. Collective representation at Community level

International union bodies have existed for many years, the oldest being the International Trade Secretariats (now based in Geneva). The 60s, however, saw the establishment of a number of bodies at European level:

- ECFTU (European Confederation of Free Trade Unions) covers 11 million Community workers, 3 million of whom form the EMF (European Metalworkers Federation) — so far the most active European union organisation. ECFTU is social-democrat in leaning, and the TUC may affiliate.
- European organisation of the World Federation of Labour covers only Benelux and France, with c. 2.5 million members
- CGT-CGIL Permanent Liaison Secretariat — the Franco-Italian Communist unions remained aloof for many years from the E.E.C., but have now changed their policy. They represent some 4 million members.

The ECFTU member federations maintain close links with the international (world-wide) organisations such as the International Metalworkers Federation (IMF) and the International Confederation of Chemical and General Workers Unions (ICF). The activities of these bodies are mainly aimed at multinational companies — particularly US-owned multinationals — and take two notable forms. Firstly, a great deal of lobbying goes on to achieve their aims through international organisations (GATT, OECD, ILO and E.E.C.); and secondly, through sector and company councils — on a world or European basis — the IMF, ICF add EMF attempt to co-ordinate the bargaining activities of a company's employees in all operating countries in order to reach a position where they can negotiate centrally with the company. In general, this policy has borne more fruit with European multinationals than with US-owned ones. The EMF already holds talks, if not negotiations, with companies such as Philips, Fokker-VFW, Brown Boveri & Cie etc.

Part 3. The effect on British employment and industrial relations of E. E. C. entry

15. The effect on British employment and industrial relations of E. E. C. entry

Employment and free movement

As from 1st January 1973, the provisions of Articles 48 and 49, and the 1968 Regulation (1612/68) apply in Great Britain but not in Northern Ireland. Nationals of E.E.C. countries are able 'to enter another country to seek work, or to take up a job waiting for them, merely on the presentation of a passport or an identity card. They do not need work permits and must be allowed access to employment on equal terms with nationals of the country they have entered — except in the case of employment in public administration. They are also entitled to equal treatment in relation to remuneration, working conditions, access to housing and property, vocational training and retraining, social security and trade union rights' (Department of Employment).

The Regulations covering E.E.C. nationals entering Britain have been published by HMSO (509: 'Statement of Immigration Rules for Control on Entry'; and 510; 'Statement of Immigration Rules for Control after Entry'). The relevant provisions are as follows:

'Control on Entry

Part V. Nationals of E.E.C. Countries

Introductory

'52. On the accession of the United Kingdom to the European Economic Community nationals of member countries (Belgium, Denmark, France, and Federal Republic of Germany, Italy, Luxembourg and the Netherlands) acquire greater freedom of entry than hitherto. This Part of the rules makes special provision for the admission of nationals of those countries. In cases to which these special provisions apply, they override the foregoing provisions of these rules.

'53. In the following paragraphs E.E.C. national means a national of one of the other member countries of the Community listed in *paragraph 52*, except that a passenger who is —

(a)   a national of the Netherlands solely by birth in or other connection with Surinam or the Antilles, or

(b)   a national of France solely by birth in or other connection with one of the French overseas dependent territories

is not on that account to be regarded as an E.E.C. national.

General

'54. When an E.E.C. national is given leave to enter, no condition is to be imposed restricting his employment or occupation in the United Kingdom. Admission should normally be for a period of 6 months, except in the case of a returning resident or the holder of a valid residence permit.

Workers, businessmen and self-employed persons

'55. An E.E.C. national who wishes to enter the United Kingdom in order to take or seek employment, set up in business or work as a self-employed person is to be admitted without a work permit or other prior consent.

Dependents

'56. When a passenger is admitted in accordance with *paragraph 55*, the member of his family accompanying him should be given leave to enter for the same period. His family should be regarded as consisting of his wife, their children under 21, their other children if still dependent, and their dependent parents and grandparents.

'57. Members of the family (as defined in *paragraph 56*) of an E.E.C. national who has previously been admitted under *paragraph 55* should be given leave to enter in order to join him in the United Kingdom.

'Control after Entry

Section II. Nationals of E.E.C. Countries

Workers, businessmen and self-employed persons

'37. If a person admitted for 6 months enters employment he should be issued with a residence permit. The residence permit should be limited to the duration of the employment if this is expected to be less than 12 months. Otherwise the permit should be for 5 years. But a permit should not normally be granted if the person has not found employment at the end of the 6 months' period for which he was admitted, nor if during that time he has become a charge on public funds.

'38. If a person admitted for 6 months produces evidence by the end of that period that he has established himself in business or in a self-employed occupation he should be issued with a residence permit for 5 years. Otherwise, depending on the circumstances, he may be refused a residence permit, or he may be granted a short extension of his stay in order to complete arrangements for establishing himself in business or a self-employed occupation.

'39. The duration of a residence permit should be curtailed if it is evident that the holder is living on public funds although capable of maintaining himself.

'40. A person issued with a residence permit for 5 years should have the time limit on his stay removed after he has remained here for 4 years in employment, in business or as a self-employed person, unless, in the light of all the relevant circumstances of the case, including those set out in *paragraphs 4 and 39,* there are grounds for not removing the time limit. If the time limit is not then removed, the case should be reviewed on the expiry of the residence permit. In the case of a person issued with a residence permit for employment, a renewal limited to 12 months may be appropriate if he has been unemployed for more than 12 consecutive months during the previous 5 years.

Families

'41. Members of the family of a person to whom *paragraphs 37 to 40* apply should be granted extensions of stay or issued with residence permits in the same terms as those relating to that person at the time in question. The family should be regarded as consisting of the person's wife, their children under 21, their other dependent children, and their dependent parents and grandparents.

Settlement

'42. The time limit on the stay of the following categories of persons should be removed;

(a)   a person who has been continuously resident in the United Kingdom for at least 3 years, has been in employment in the United Kingdom or any other member country of the European Economic Community for the preceding 12 months, and has reached the age of entitlement to a State retirement pension:

(b)   a person who has ceased to be employed owing to a permanent incapacity for work arising out of an accident at work or an occupational disease entitling him to a State disability pension;

(c)   a person who has been continuously resident in the United Kingdom for more than 2 years, and who has ceased to be employed owing to a permanent incapacity for work;

(d)   any member of the family (see *paragraph 41)* of a person in category (a), (b) or (c) above;

(e)   any member of the family of a person who, after residing continuously in the United Kingdom for at least 2 years, dies as the result of an accident at work or an accupational disease.'

Note: paragraph 4 (referred to in paragraph 40 above) reads:

'General considerations

4.   The succeeding paragraphs set out the main categories of people who may be given limited leave to enter and who may seek variation of their leave, and the principles to be followed in dealing with their applications, or in initiating any variation of their leave. In deciding these matters account is to be taken of all the relevant facts; the fact

that the applicant satisfies the formal requirements of these rules for stay, or further stay, in the proposed capacity is not conclusive in his favour. It will, for example, be relevant whether the person has observed the time limit and conditions subject to which he was admitted; whether in the light of his character, conduct or associations it is undesirable to permit him to remain; whether he represents a danger to national security; or whether, if allowed to remain for the period for which he wishes to stay, he might not be returnable to another country.'

It will be noted that the main presumption is still that E.E.C. nationals enter for the purposes of *employment*. Fears that unemployed E.E.C. nationals will become a burden on public funds are, on the basis of the Regulations, unfounded. Even after he has received the five-year permit, he may find renewal limited to 12 months if he has been unemployed (para. 40, *510*).

Despite the free movement provisions, immigration into Britain from E.E.C. countries may well be insignificant. The effect of similar provisions in the Six has been limited (see Table on page 122), and over the last 20 years intra-E.E.C. movement has even decreased. On the face of it, Britain has no special attractions for Continental workers, since earnings in other parts of Europe are at least as high, social security benefits more favourable, and Britain's industrial relations reputation may well actively militate against the movement of labour into the UK.

Wages and labour cost

The level of wages in the UK lies, in real terms, about midway down the scale at present. Rates of growth, however, are considerably lower: it nevertheless seems unlikely that comparative or parity claims with other European countries will be pursued except in isolated cases (e.g. multinational companies).

Conditions, however, are a different matter. The author is aware of at least one claim citing the conditions of Japanese female electronics workers, and comparisons with other European countries are frequently made when an increased holiday entitlement is being sought. Holiday claims usually fail to mention that most countries work longer weekly hours, so that total hours worked annually are within the same fairly narrow band in all European countries. The situation will be somewhat different by 1974, when nearly all Community countries will be operating a 40-hour week. Shiftwork, overtime and nightwork premiums are at least as favourable in Britain, and in most cases more so.

Total labour cost per worker is remarkably comparable in all countries: and where in Denmark and Britain direct wages make up a much higher percentage of total cost, this relates to the fact that in both countries social security is financed by relatively low direct contributions and large-scale participation of the central exchequer. In the Six, social security is almost wholly financed by employer and employee contributions.

The problems of making the different social security systems compatible, let alone harmonizing them, is a considerable one. The coverage is the same. The differences arise from methods of financing and administering them. The new social security legislation in Britain, interestingly, moves slightly nearer to the general European trend both in its earnings-related provisions and in that it provides for supplementary schemes and funds to be set up occupationally — a system which exists in a number of countries, where the funds are in some cases administered by joint bodies representing both sides of industry. This would no doubt be feasible in Britain, if it were desirable, but there are no signs as yet that the nettle will be grasped to any significant extent.

It may be noted that social security *benefits* in other European countries tend to be appreciably higher than the wholly unrealistic provisions of the British system.

Industrial reorganization and retraining

The reformed European Social Fund together with other parts of the new co-ordinated policies could well be of major benefit to companies and workers in Britain. The Community is strongly aware of the importance of regional and other disparities (see the Social Policy Guidelines) which in any case represent a threat to the expansion of free competition. The financial means of the Community funds may be used either in conjunction with Government redevelopment or retraining schemes (such as the one recently announced by the UK Government) or those initiated by industry with Community approval.

Effect on UK industrial relations

So far, the existence of the E.E.C. has had no major effect on the social or industrial relations structures of its member countries. Indeed, these countries have known rapid developments in their legislation and collective agreements, yet the degree of Community co-ordination in these developments has been minimal, and national solutions continue to be sought for purely national problems. The entry of three new members, representing at least two cultural traditions in addition to those already represented in the Six, will serve to complicate this situation still further. Nevertheless, there have been certain general trends which have appeared in one form or another throughout Europe (but with a distinct national flavour in each case); and if the institutions of the Community are to attempt any harmonization in the field of industrial relations and there is a clear will to do so, it can reasonably be expected that these trends will constitute their starting point.

In immediate terms however, no substantial change can be expected to influence UK industrial relations. But the strong involvement of the TUC and the major British unions in the European union bodies, which exists and can be expected to develop, together with the present trend towards a greater influence of European trade unions in the Community's policy-making institutions, may guarantee the development of European policies which will ultimately affect individual countries. (The inclusion of the provisions of the SE statute on worker representation at board level into the draft Fifth Directive on company law is a first example of the possibilities of this tendency.)

It can be anticipated with some confidence that the catalyst for the development of such union policies will be the question of multinational companies (also the subject of much recent discussion at ILO and OECD), and that this will include the larger question of Community control over such companies' financial and personnel activities. One foretaste of this has been the proposal to harmonize periods of notice and other arrangements in cases of dismissal and redundancy, on the basis that multinationals have had a tendency to try to exploit the existing differences in national legislations. A more fundamental foretaste has been the debate on the European company, a debate which is only just beginning in earnest, and at the root of which is the question of ownership and control of industry and capital.

This question is also fundamental to the ideological differences of approach which could potentially cause a major split between European unions (a split along the lines of what has recently been seen in the British Labour Party). On the one hand, the trade unions in a number of countries affirm their co-operation and co-responsibility within a free-enterprise capitalist economy, and seek powers of co-decision within its framework and institutions. In the Six, this social-democrat approach characterizes the German, Luxembourg, Belgian and part of the French and Dutch trade union movement.

To these can now be added the Danes. On the other hand, the Italian unions, and the French Communists, despite their recent formalised overtures to the Community's institutions in Brussels, fundamentally reject such co-operation within the 'system'.

While the controlling feature of the British Labour Party probably lies nearer to the social-democrat, consensus, group, certain British unions have more in common with the other tendency. Certainly the Institute for Workers' Control would not countenance any kind of 'consensus' co-operation, and the IWC is not inadequately represented in the leadership of some of the largest British unions.

It is of fundamental importance to the Commission's plans that Europe's unions should, as a whole, decide which way they are going to fall. Nevertheless, they are unlikely to find a common accord. The Commission's proposals for both the SE statute and the harmonization of company law and worker representation are dependent upon a co-operative approach by all sides involved, and they are unlikely to get overall consensus. But in a sense it is useful that the SE draft has brought up these questions at an early stage, for a number of problems currently under discussion in most countries revolve around them.

Probably the most important problem exercising British — and Italian — industrial relations at the moment is closely connected with the principle of co-operation, and also illuminates the problems which Community 'social policy' will meet: the development of orderly bargaining structures. Both Britain and Italy suffer from a formal system of collective bargaining which is wholly unrepresentative of actual events in the plant, not so much in the sense that informal plant bargaining takes place as in that the representational structure of trade unions and employers' organisations has never been properly defined. There is no clear definition of exactly what shall be negotiated by whom at what level. The Industrial Relations Act has sought one kind of solution to a part of this problem (arguably the wrong one: the 'bargaining unit' does not help the 'development of strong representative trade unions' very much, and it is the latter which is essential in a 'European' context*). But its provisions are probably not as significant as the fact that it has brought some matters to the fore which had not only never been adequately discussed but, in many cases, would not normally have occurred to the majority of people on both sides of industry and outside; and there is probably a readiness to consider change. Nobody would consider that a bald dictate from Brussels could

---

*) The introduction of the Continental concept of 'most representative societies' at national level might have been more effective and would certainly have prevented the willy-nilly registration of a host of tinpot unions.

institute reform, least of all those in Brussels. It is obvious that both Britain and Italy will have to solve their problems each in its national context. But it may be possible now to consider the application of European experience, where it has proved itself, to the British context, even if it results in ultimate rejection.

Whatever solutions are chosen, or tried, however, will have great relevance to matters such as the European company, or harmonized legislation, or European collective agreements. If these policies are to be developed at Community level, they must be supported by reasonable possibilities of implementation at the level of the country or industry. In terms of the UK, this can be guaranteed only if a realistic and carefully considered restructuring of collective bargaining can be developed, to which the parties (in European terms: the 'social *partners*') can adhere. It has never been a tradition in Britain to seek 'structures' as such for industrial relations. But it may now be time to do so, and membership of the E.E.C. may provide a stimulus to examine other people's industrial relations frameworks.

Two points might seem worth considering. The first concerns the comprehensiveness of the industrial relations framework. A brief examination of the sections of this book on the individual countries will show that in general the countries with the most detailed arrangements for collective bargaining and employer/employee relations are those which in recent years have enjoyed the least strife. The second point relates to those countries which now maintain what has been termed a 'co-operative' approach to these questions; it is observable that such countries have all conceded to unions and employees – by legislation or collective agreement, and through a variety of institutions and 'spheres of influence', considerably greater and more formalised rights of co-decision in either the management of the company as a whole or in particular areas of day-to-day management which are of greatest importance to employees. These areas include influence on safety and hygiene provisions, but also on dismissals, major reorganisations of production, questions of payment systems etc. Obviously, co-decision already operates in practice in large sections of British industry. But in the UK this is not based on specific rights, but on *de facto* rights at most, and there is a world of difference between the one type and the other as far as a good industrial relations atmosphere is concerned. *De facto* rights confirm again and again the function of, in particular, trade unions as strugglers against capitalism, wresting rights from an unwilling employer on behalf of the lads. Whether this is a useful attitude in the 70s is a matter of opinion.

The Continental method of institutionalising co-decision and consultation rights usually takes the form of a works council. The existence of such a body is, from an employer's point-of-view, a useful tool and in the past considerably aided the exponents of divide-and-rule. On the one hand it is seen to be representative of all employees, and not only union-members; it is limited to one plant or one company; and in every case it owes some duty of loyalty to the firm. On the other hand it obliges trade unionists who are members of the works council to appear as members of the works council and not as agents of a trade union — and until very recently trade unions as such had few rights of access to the plant, their functions lying at higher levels of negotiation. In recent years, therefore, 'industrial democracy' has tended to mean as much 'increased union rights in the plant' as 'increased co-decision' in Continental countries. It is important to remember that the framework of industrial relations in the Six in general specifies the subjects on which unions may negotiate and the appropriate level for each subject. It is not normal, for example, (exception: Italy) for such key issues as wages to be agreed at domestic level. The (relatively homogeneous) conception of 'industrial democracy' in the Six is clearly at odds with what is meant by the same phrase in the UK. There is perhaps some truth in the assertion that their 'industrial democracy' = our 'dynamic (i.e. plant-level) collective bargaining tradition'. But while similar in type, the two traditions are wholly different in practice, and to find common ground, as the Community no doubt will have to, one must anticipate both an increase in Continental 'industrial democracy' and the development of a more orderly framework in the UK. Nevertheless, in concrete terms, the principle of upwards harmonization and the Community's generally socialising effect (in every sense of the word) may well mean that managerial prerogatives will be a major area of change in the next few years.

In many respects, of which social policy is one, the enlarged Community cannot be compared with its predecessor. The industrial relations traditions of the new members are even less compatible with those of the Six than those of the Six were with each other, and, in formulating European policies, the Commission (among others) will need to re-think its present proposals. What has been said in earlier paragraphs of this section is intended to spotlight some of the issues which will need to be closely examined in the future rather than to pinpoint specific 'effects' which UK membership might incur. Britain will of necessity participate in the development of social policies: what has appeared so far can, in the future, represent only a starting-point. Nothing has been irrevocably decided in this sphere as yet, and there is every likelihood, as well as some need, for Community thinking to be re-shaped to take into account the interests of Denmark, Eire and the UK. It may be, also, that the institutions of the Community as at present constituted are not the best forum for the discussion of these problems. Social policy lagged behind other questions for most of the 15 years of the Six, and even now is being formulated to meet predominantly economic requirements. It is to be hoped that when the social policy programme has been drafted, it will be made widely available and will be flexible enough to take into account the long-term implications of any action at European level on this fundamentally important subject.

To add another item to the endless catalogue of 'new opportunities' which Community membership may bring: those involved in industrial relations in Britain may derive more advantages from looking at domestic problems in a Community setting than from continuing to refer solely to the home front.

Special Appendix: Norway

Employment

Recruitment

There are no specific regulations affecting recruitment in Norway: the employer may recruit as he thinks fit. However, the State operates a national employment service. Commercial manpower and employment agencies are prohibited.

Scandinavian workers are treated as Norwegian workers in terms of recruitment and residence. All other aliens however require an offer of employment and a work permit before entry.

Contract of employment

The Norwegian contract of employment is concluded for an indefinite period, and may contain an initial probationary period. Its terms are in most cases laid down by collective agreement.

Termination — dismissal — redundancy

The contract is terminated by notice. There are legally determined minimum periods of notice:

manual (hourly, daily, weekly and piece-rated)	14 days
non-manual	1 month from the end of the calendar month

These periods are increased for

employees aged 50 (with at least 10 year's service)	2 months
employees aged 60 (with at least 10 year's service)	3 months

Employees may not be dismissed during maternity leave, nor during absence due to sickness or accident up to 3 months (for employees with 2 years' service after age 20). or 1 year (for employees with 10 years'service after age 20).

Employees cannot be dismissed without good reason. If an employee considers himself wrongly dismissed, he may take his complaint to court. Reinstatement and/or compensation may be awarded if 'dismissal is not warranted by the circumstances of the owner of the establishment, the employee, or the establishment'. Proceedings cannot be instituted however if the dismissal resulted from pressure applied by other employees, which would have caused damage had the employer not yielded.

Severance pay is provided for under a generally applicable collective agreement. This is financed through a fund to which the employer contributes, and provides a payment of 2,500 kr. for employees over 50 years of age, with 10 years' service and who have been covered by the scheme for 3 months before dismissal: this rises to 7,000 kr. at age 65.

Industrial relations

Industrial relations in Norway are highly centralised, as might be expected of a country with a relatively small population. But the system is very much a voluntary one: beyond providing a framework for collective bargaining, the Government does not intervene except in times of major crisis.

Trade unions

Organization is fairly high in Norway — about 63% of the working population. In some sectors it is much higher; in engineering, mining, building and transport some 90% of manual workers are members of a union; 90% of supervisors; but only 30% - 40% of non-manual employees. Unions in the main organize a single branch of industry, but there are a number of craft unions, ranging from woodworkers (5,788) through industrial journalists (458) to prompters (18, all female). The main union organisation in Norway, however, is the confederation *LO (Landsorganisjonen i Norge)*. Through its member unions, LO represents almost 600,000.

Employers' associations

The main employers' organisation is *NAF (Norsk Arbeidsgiver-
forening/*Norwegian Employers' Confederation). NAF is formed of
associations for each branch of industry; but, as with the unions, the
main functions of collective bargaining are undertaken by the
confederation.

Collective bargaining

Collective bargaining mainly concerns wages. A number of matters
which are negotiated in other countries are the subject of legislation
in Norway, including hours of work and holidays.

Every two years, a model agreement is reached between the
central bargaining partners NAF and LO. It is preceded by tripartite consultations which attempt to establish guidelines for wages
and prices in general. The model is then either applied or is used as a
framework in agreements for individual branches of industry. These
tend to include special arrangements to suit the conditions prevailing in, say, the building industry.

If negotiations break down, mediation must be attempted: the
chief State mediator is empowered to order a cooling-off period of
at least 14 days. If mediation fails, the parties may submit the
dispute to voluntary arbitration, but this is rare, although it was
used in 1972. In certain cases the Government may impose obligatory
arbitration — this has been applied only two or three times in the
last ten years.

Disputes on the application of a collective agreement are dealt
with by a Labour Court consisting of a neutral Chairman, two
representatives of the public interest, and two each of employers'
and unions' representatives.

Wage agreements differ according to sector as to the type of
provision: the engineering agreement lays down minimum wages
for 3 skill categories with the express understanding that these will be
improved upon in individual agreements. The majority of Norwegian
workers are covered by a standard wage system, which fixes hourly
rates. For the construction sector, national piece rates are agreed.
A certain degree of wage drift has become usual, and a compen-
sating increase is included in standard wage agreements and others
where a certain amount of drift is not achieved. Index-linking clauses
are also usual, since 1970.

While only members of the contracting parties are bound by the
terms of a collective agreement, the majority of employers pay the
'union rate'.

Wages, therefore, are negotiated in an orderly but flexible system at national level. Despite the existence of some (small) craft-based unions, negotiation on behalf of sectional interests at plant level is unknown: any variation on the collective agreement is a matter for individual arrangement between the employee and the employer.

Conditions of Employment

Remuneration

Wages in Norway have risen by 33% in real terms since 1964 (1971 E.E.C. figures): the current rate is around 5% annually (discounting a massive increase in the retail price index in 1970 which followed the introduction of VAT). It has already been noted that the majority of Norwegian employees are paid standard rates or piecework. There is a growing tendency towards job evaluated structures – the general guidelines for which have been the subject of a NAF/LO agreement – and away from piecework. Nevertheless, in 1969 a NAF study showed that 56% of all hours worked by men, and 53% of those worked by women were paid at piecerates.

Hours of work are legally fixed at 42½ per week, maximum 9 per day. These are standard, although office staff in manufacturing tend to work a 37-40 hour week, and employees on a 2 or 3-shift system in engineering now have a 40-hour week. Most of industry works a 5-day week. Overtime is limited to 250 hours p.a., and is illegal for employees under the age of 18. The legal minimum overtime payment is 25% bonus: by agreement it is usually 35% or 40% for the first two hours and 50% thereafter.

Annual holidays

Holidays are laid down by law at 4 weeks, of which 18 days should in principle be taken between 16th May and 30th September. Legislation provides for a complex system of holiday credits by the purchase of stamps, but a NAF/LO system, which gives additional holiday pay of slightly over 10% of average earnings, is simpler to operate.

Public holidays

Norway has 10 paid public holidays:

New Year's Day	Ascension Day
Maundy Thursday	Whit Monday
Good Friday	Christmas Day
Easter Monday	Boxing Day
May Day	National holiday

Social security

Norway has a comprehensive national insurance scheme, covering retirement, death, sickness, disability, maternity, industrial accident and disease, and family allowances. All except the last were brought under a single system in 1971, requiring a single contribution from the employer of 13% of payroll. The employee pays 7.8% (also at 1971 rates) and the central Government and the municipality each contribute 2.25%. Although contributions as a whole have risen since 1969, coverage has not, and for reasons of comparison the Tables below are given, relating to 1969. The second Table is a recalculation of the first under the main headings of the EEC breakdown, and can give only a very broad comparison.

Indirect costs as a % of direct wages

	manual %	non-manual %
Statutory costs		
paid leave	10.00	10.00
public holidays	3.50	3.60
sick pay	0.20	2.00
other pay for time not worked	0.10	0.20
national insurance contributions	8.70	8.50
other public insurance contributions	4.20	2.70
TOTAL, STATUTORY COSTS	26.40	26.90
Contractual and voluntary \costs		
employees' contributions to public insurance paid by employer	0.00	0.20
contributions to private pension systems	0.70	4.60
private pensions and related benefits	0.60	2.40
private sickness insurance schemes	0.10	0.00
private industrial accident insurance	0.10	0.10
company doctors	0.30	0.30
cloakrooms, bathrooms	0.30	0.10
meal subsidy	0.60	0.70
transport	0.20	0.10
housing	0.70	1.00
training	0.60	0.70
leisure activities	0.20	0.20
clothing	0.60	0.20
payment in kind	0.10	0.10
other	0.40	0.40
TOTAL, CONTRACTUAL & VOLUNTARY COSTS	5.80	11.10
TOTAL INDIRECT LABOUR COST	32.20	38.00

(Source: NAF)

Recalculation on E.E.C. model

	manual %	non-manual %
1. Direct wages and regular bonuses }	75.67	72.48
2. Other bonuses and *ex gratia* payments }		
3. Payment for days not worked	10.28	10.00
4. Social security contributions	11.04	14.78
5. Payments in kind	0.07	0.07
6. Other payments of a social nature	2.49	2.17
7. Training costs	0.45	0.50
8. Social taxes	—	—
	100.00	100.00

Employee Representation

Supervisory Boards

As from 1973, companies with more than 200 employees are required to establish a Supervisory Board which has the ultimate power of decision on 'investments of considerable size compared with the company's capital' and on matters connected with 'rationalization and reorganisation within the company leading to major changes in the disposition of the labour force'. One-third of the Supervisory Board will consist of representatives elected by and from the personnel. This obligation will also exist in companies with 50-200 employees if a majority of the labour force so decides.

Works Council

Establishments with more than 100 employees must set up a joint works council with equal management and employee representation. The Chair rotates between the groups. The council has a right to propose improvements in safety arrangements and general working conditions, and changes in training policy. It must also be informed about the economic situation of the firm, and must be consulted on decisions which will have a major effect on the labour force.

Shop stewards

2-10 shop stewards may be appointed for each trade union represented in the plant, according to the size of the establishment. Stewards are under an obligation to maintain industrial peace under the collective agreements. Their functions include dealing with disputes arising from the application of agreements, and they have a right to be consulted on the works rules when these are determined.

Bibliography

E.E.C. (All EC policy material is available from HMSO

    Treaty of Rome — official translation

    Treaty of Accession

    European Communities Secondary Legislation — part 10: social affairs (includes Regulations on movement of labour, transferability of social security, reform of European Social Fund etc.)

    Proposed Statute for the European Company (1970 version)

    Preliminary Guidelines for a Social Policy Programme in the Community (1971 — the Coppé Memorandum)

E.E.C. Statistics (from Statistical Office of the European Communities, via HMSO)

    Earnings, hours of work and numbers employed: harmonized Community series (Social Statistics — yellow)

    Sample survey of the labour force (1971)

    Labour cost — 1969 enquiry (preliminary results)

Note: new harmonized series covering the Nine will be forthcoming from the Statistical Office of the European Communities. The enquiries and the sample surveys are the forerunners of direct enquiries on which statistical series will be based in future.

Useful publications covering all Community countries.

    Employers' Liabilities Under Social Service Legislation in the Countries of the European Common Market with quarterly supplements.
    CED Samson, 7 Philippe de Champagnestreet, 1000 BRUSSELS, Belgium.
    (Extremely useful, English slightly hairraising but comprehensible).

    European Labour Relations in the 70s — Part I: An Overview; Part II: UK, Sweden and the E.E.C. countries — 1972
    Management Counselors International S.A., 209a, Avenue Louise, 1050 BRUSSELS, Belgium.
    (Part I contains much useful material written by a senior E.E.C. official, by the Secretary-General of the European Metalworkers' Federation on the European Company, and by the Director of the ILO's Institute of International Labour Studies on worker participation.)

    Labour Relations and Employment Conditions in the European Economic Community — 1972
    Coventry and District Engineering Employers' Association
    (Good background work, excellent statistics and assessment of Community developments, but less reliable on individual countries)

    Western European Labor and the American Corporation ed. Alfred Kamin — 1970 Bureau of National Affairs Inc., Washington
    (Large. Contributions from European experts especially valuable)

Trade Unions

    The Trade Union Movement in the European Community (Dossier) — 1972
    E.E.C. Press and Information Directorate

    White-Collar Trade Unions by Adolf Sturmthal 1966
    University of Illinois, Urbana
    see also the *Management Counselors International* publications

Employee Participation
Workers' Participation in Western Europe IPM Information Report No. 10
(New Series) — 1971
Institute of Personnel Management, London

*Company and Corporation Reform and Worker Participation: the State of
the debate* by Michael P. Fogarty
in *British Journal of Industrial Relations* Vol.X No. 1 March 1972 (A useful
antidote to the Germanic view which has dominated this debate)

Mensualisation, Integration, Staff Status
Staff status for manual workers by Terry Robinson — 1972
Kogan Page, London
(Contains a useful description of the situation in Europe)

Information

United Kingdom

> Department of Employment
> 8 St. James's Square,
> London S.W.1
> Tel.: (01) 930 6200
> Statistics: Watford 28508

> Department of Trade and Industry,
> EEC/Efta Information Unit,
> 1 Victoria Street,
> London S.W.1
> Tel.: (01) 222 7877

> European Communities Information Office
> 23 Chesham Street,
> London S.W.1
> Tel.: (01) 235 4904

E.E.C. Commission

> Commission of the European Communities, (Directorate-General V —
> 200 rue de la Loi,   Social Affairs)
> 1040 Brussels,
> Belgium.
> Tel.: Brussels 350040 and 358040

> Statistics: Directorate E (Social Statistics)
> Statistical Office of the European Communities,
> Centre Europeen,
> Kirchberg,
> Luxembourg
>
> Tel.: Luxembourg 47941

Index